Ex Libris

Kindest regards,
Manly P. Hall

Manly P. Hall illustrated by Jessica Naomi

Manly P. Hall A Seeker of More Intelligent Life – Book First

Compiled with graphics and edits by Darrell Jordan, Copyright © First Edition 2023. All rights reserved.

No part of this book may be reproduced in whole or in part without the written permission from the publisher, nor stored in any retrieval system or transmitted by any means, electronic, mechanical, photocopying, recording, or other, without the written consent of the publisher.

For bulk purchases, please contact the publisher.

Enquiry@Athenaia.Co

Library of Congress Cataloging-in Publication Data

Names: Hall, Manly P. | Jordan, Darrell

Title: Manly P. Hall A Seeker of More Intelligent Life – Book First

Description: First U.S. edition. | Coeur D'Alene, Idaho: Athenaia [2023]

Identifiers: LCCN (pending) | ISBN 979-8-88556-043-6 (First Edition hardcover)

Subjects: OCC040000: BODY, MIND & SPIRIT / Hermetism & Rosicrucianism, | PHI013000: PHILOSOPHY / Metaphysics, | SOC038000: SOCIAL SCIENCE / Freemasonry & Secret Societies

LC record available at https://lccn. loc.gov

On the internet: Parallel47North.com/collections/esoteric-books

Managing Editor: Darrell Jordan
Original Author and Essay: Manly P. Hall
Executive Producer: Yuka Jordan
Book Cover Art and Illustrations: Jessica Naomi
Image Credits: Manly P. Hall's personal collection
Printed and bound in the United States

Publisher: Athenaia, LLC

2370 N Merritt Crk Lp, Ste 1

Coeur D'Alene, ID 83814

The United States

Manly P. Hall

A Seeker of More Intelligent Life

Book First

Darrell Jordan, MPS

CONTENTS

INTRODUCTION	9
MAY 1, 1934	11
JUNE 1, 1934	16
THOUGHTS FROM A PHILOSOPHER'S SCRAPBOOK	22
JULY 1, 1934	23
THOUGHTS FROM A PHILOSOPHER'S SCRAPBOOK	29
AUGUST 1, 1934	29
THOUGHTS FROM A PHILOSOPHER'S SCRAPBOOK	34
SEPTEMBER 1, 1934	36
SOME PHILOSOPHICAL FRAGMENTS	42
HEALING - CHAPTER I	42
PALINGENESIS OF PLANTS	45
OCTOBER 1, 1934	48
HEALING - CHAPTER II	55
NOVEMBER 1, 1934	61
HEALING - CHAPTER III	67
DECEMBER 1, 1934	74
THE MASTERY OF FEAR - I	80
JANUARY 1, 1935	87
THE MASTERY OF FEAR - II	93
A LITTLE ESSAY ON BEAUTY	98
PARIS, FEBRUARY 1, 1935	100
THE FIRST PRINCIPLES OF SUPERSCIENCE - I	110
LONDON, MARCH 1, 1935	113
THE FIRST PRINCIPLES OF SUPERSCIENCE - II	122
NEW YORK, APRIL 1, 1935	126
AUTHOR AND MANAGING EDITOR	139
MANLY P. HALL BOOK SERIES	141

INTRODUCTION

EDITOR'S NOTE

Manly Hall was born on 18 March 1901, in Peterborough, Canada, to William S. and Louise Palmer Hall. The Hall family moved to Sioux Falls, South Dakota, United States, in 1904. Manly Hall later settled in Los Angeles in 1919.

As a young man, he became interested in all forms of occult subjects. He subsequently joined a number of societies, among them the Theosophical Society, the Freemasons, the Societas Rosecruciana in Civitatibus Foederatis, and the American Federation of Astrologers.

In 1922, Hall wrote his first book: Initiates of the Flame and was collecting all form of esoteric/exoteric/mystical subject matter, in his own words: "late in the fall of 1922, the plan for a comprehensive work on the symbolism of western mystical societies began to take shape in my mind. It soon became apparent that research facilities for such a project were not available in Southern California... The only answer was to contact antiquarian book dealers and elicit their cooperation in the search for the items desired." In 1934, Hall founded the Philosophical Research Society, a research institute modeled on the ancient school of Pythagoras.

He was ordained a minister in 1923 to an occult/mystic congregation at the Church of the People in California. In that same year specifically in May 1923, Manly Hall began the membership/student based, not for sale magazine, all written, edited and published by Hall titled the "The All Seeing-Eye."

We now follow Manly P. Hall from the "All Seeing Eye" book series at the age of 24, to his private lessons for his students in this latest book series, at the age of 32. In this series, Mr. Hall moves from imparting wisdom through stories to a confident, fact-based approach of his findings and understanding of his research. His elucidation exudes confidence and is well written, with it being exceedingly broad in scope. In this series we provide 4 years of lessons condensed into four books. We are positive you will find the information herein to be quite useful in filling in some hidden areas of understanding in religion and history.

Editing was minimal in terms of punctuation and spelling. In some cases, there are made-up words (or words that are no longer in use) in which case they were left spelled as is.

I'm sure that you will find, as did I, that Manly Hall was highly intelligent and possibly bordering on genius. Suffice it to say, we are positive you will enjoy the many journeys Manly Hall takes you on.

Darrell Jordan, MPS

MAY 1, 1934

Dear Friend,

Nearly fourteen years have passed since I began writing and lecturing on philosophy and metaphysics. During these years, I have delivered several thousand lectures and published some forty hoops and essays. Students of occultism, comparative religion and kindred subjects throughout the world have honored me with their support and confidence. The years have brought an ever-increasing demand for the organization and classification of my ideas and teachings so that the average person can make fuller use thereof as the foundation for a personal code of more intelligent living.

During the prosperous periods preceding the present social crisis people were so obsessed by economics that few concerned themselves with the deeper issues of life. As adversity becomes general, however, sober thinking comes into fashion. When our systems fail us, we must finally come to depend upon ourselves for security and well-being. It has been demonstrated throughout history that learning is restored in trying times and ignored during prosperous interludes.

If the philosophical doctrines which I have been promulgating were my own or had been derived from the prejudices and conceits of untrained and incompetent minds, I would have small courage for their perpetuation. It has been wisely observed that "opinionism is a falling sickness of the mind." It is far from my intention to burden an opinion ridden world with more ill-digested speculation. The fallacies of perverse thought are everywhere apparent and the absence of a mature mental approach to the great problems of the day is observable in every department of society. When, however, I know that the substance of my teachings has been drawn from the most mature reflections of the world's ablest and most profound thinkers and is justified by thousands of years of test and application, I am inspired, even compelled by an inner impulse, to devote my time and energy to the dissemination of these teachings.

It is this inner conviction of the paramount importance of spiritual and philosophical education in these uncertain times which has sustained me through the numerous vicissitudes of past years. The knowledge which I have derived from my almost continuous researches into the "divine science of living" is so priceless an asset in these troubled days that I feel it a duty as well as a privilege to pass on the results of my researches as a working formula for a useful and intelligent life. The average man or woman has neither the time nor the training necessary to gather from the experience of the ages the substance from which to evolve an enlightened personal philosophy, yet such a personal philosophy is absolutely essential to the mental and spiritual well-being of the individual. A man is what he thinks. His mental attitude is the key to his code of action, and civilization is fundamentally a code of action. According to Cicero, the purpose of civilization is to bring the human family to an enlightened and cooperative state. This highly desirable condition is only possible when men themselves are enlightened.

> "ETERNAL REASON, CREATOR OF ALL THINGS, THE MAN THOU HATH FASHIONED IN THY WISDOM AWAITS THE WORK THOU WOULDST HAVE HIM DO." - The Prayer of Hermes.

In every age, sages and prophets, philosophers and priests, have sought by example and word to educate and inspire mankind in the essentials of enlightened living. The lives of these heroic souls are perpetuated in the scriptures and classics of every nation and their words are preserved as a vast literature in the great libraries of the world. The British Museum alone has nearly fifty miles of bookshelves. Locked within its ancient volumes are the accumulated ideals and inspirations of the race. Having inherited so much of wisdom, is it not amazing that we remain so unwise? that possessing as we do so much of that which is good and noble, we remain unrefined and ignoble?

Is it strange then that a great man like DeQuincy should sit weeping in the British Museum, saddened by the realization that he could not live long enough to read all of these books and share with all the dreamers of the past their vision for human improvement? Yet DeQuincy has left us a formula, derived from his despair: "As I cannot read all books," he said, "I will read only the best!"

The first step in the organization of thought, therefore, is to reduce the complexity of knowledge to a more or less simple program and to discover from the whole philosophical literature of the race those parts which are of primary significance. He who uses this process will soon discover that beneath a vast and complex philosophical literature are a few basic principles. These principles, once grasped, equip the mind to cope with any issue with at least a fair measure of true intelligence.

The last fifteen years of my life have been devoted to an examination and classification of essential learning. During this time, my research has covered over forty great systems of religion and philosophy. My purpose has been to focus the light of an ageless wisdom upon the problems of today, to discover, if possible, from those who have lived well the secret of right living, from those who have thought well the secret of right thinking, and from those who have acted nobly the secret of noble action. I believe that to some measure at least I have succeeded in this effort and that I have recovered from the obscurity of centuries the essential elements of that enlightened mode of existence which Pythagoras called the "philosophic life."

If, as Plato has so nobly written, philosophy is the greatest good which the gods have ever conferred upon men, it naturally follows that the possession of it bestows the greatest wealth that any person is capable of accumulating. The philosopher only is truly great, the philosopher only is capable of being truly good, and philosophy alone contributes that immortality which must finally be the quest of every man.

You may naturally ask what I mean by philosophy, for it is evident that my use of the word is not according to the popular concept. The word philosophy was first used by Pythagoras, the greatest of the Grecian Initiates, who is accredited with having created the term. The word itself means; Friendship for or love of wisdom. A philosopher, then, is one who loves wisdom, whose life is devoted to the discovery and application of truth. That which we love we serve and a philosopher is one who loves wisdom so sincerely that he becomes its servant, obeys its laws and dedicates himself to its principles. A philosopher is not one who reads, studies or memorizes the thoughts or opinions of others, but one who so cherishes the great ideals of the race that he lives a harmless and creative life, achieving the highest axiom of the Platonists, namely.

"Wisdom is thinking WITH God and thinking WITH Nature."

You will perceive how different this is from the modern concept, for wisdom today is interpreted to be "thinking OF God and OF Nature."

According to the modern definition, philosophy covers six fields of mental activity, as follows:

1. Metaphysics, which includes theology, cosmology, and the nature of being.

2. Logic, or the doctrine of reasonableness.

3. Ethics, which includes morality and character and the discovery of the nature of good.

4. Psychology, which includes the whole field of mental phenomena.

5. Epistemology, which is concerned primarily with the problem as to whether knowledge in itself can exist in an absolute form.

6. Aesthetics, which includes the science of the reactions caused by beauty, harmony, elegance, and nobility.

This classification is excellent as far as it goes but is incomplete. Every branch of learning is susceptible of division into a septenary, its parts being under the rulership of the seven sacred planets. The seventh branch of philosophy, not given in any exoteric classification, is THEURGY, a word first used by the Alexandrian Neo-Platonists. The word theurgy means "a divine work" and was defined by the ancients as "doing the work of God." The popular translation associates the word with miracles, but it really means the science of becoming godlike and covers the actual processes by which a man becomes a philosopher, or, as the ancients called it, the disciplines of philosophy.

Thus, in its seven branches philosophy covers all of the sacred and profane forms of learning and by the possession of it the individual achieves the perfection of himself. Only by becoming a philosopher in the truest sense of that term does man fulfill the purpose of his existence. Therefore, it is our intention to devote the first twelves of these Student Letters to a summary of the principles of philosophy.

I believe that through these letters, I shall be able to accomplish a work that has been close to my heart for many years. I want to bring to everyone who is interested in self-improvement a concise and organized picture of what constitutes a philosophic life. We shall pass, step by step, through all of the departments of philosophy, from Metaphysics to Theurgy, interpreting each of them, not in the superficial way in which they are approached by modern scholastics, but according to the method advocated and practiced by those great initiated philosophers to whom we owe all that we possess of an inspired learning.

I want you to come to look upon philosophy not as an abstract and difficult word, suggesting arduous labor, but as a simple and friendly term standing for all that is good, and all that is real in knowledge. I want you to make philosophy the great work of your life. I want you to think of it as the greatest building power in society. The mastery of philosophy is the supreme accomplishment of which man is capable and the living of philosophy is the most noble of all arts.

Accompanying this letter is a little folder containing definitions of philosophy, or possibly more correctly, definitions about philosophy. These will show the high esteem in which this royal art has been held by able thinkers of both the ancient and modern worlds. To these I want to add my own definition:

Philosophy is the perfect science and the science of perfection.

It is that branch of learning devoted to the understanding and application of knowledge has as its first work the elevation of the human intellect to a realization of the divine plan. It has as its final consummation the elevation of man to absolute union with Universal Wisdom.

In the process of perfecting its disciples, philosophy makes use of every known form of knowledge and he who perfects himself in its principles becomes truly divine. As religion, philosophy leads to the knowledge of God; as philosophy it leads to the knowledge of Self; and as science, it leads to the knowledge and mastery of nature.

In the words of Paracelsus:

"The beginning of wisdom is the beginning of supernatural power."

In this present age, theology leads to confusion and science to a hopeless unbelief. Only philosophy can bring us to the Golden Time we look for. A civilization built upon ignorance and perpetuated by ignorance is collapsing under the weight of ignorance. Only from philosophy can we derive that enlightened courage with which to face the day. Those who have light within themselves will pass triumphantly through the difficult years which lie ahead. Philosophy overcomes doubt, it rescues men from despair; it perceives justice beneath injustice, and gives vision and a certain hope. By philosophy, we can live wisely and die well. The philosopher is unconquerable. The imperishable intellect survives every destruction. The philosopher is in the vanguard of progress.

Those who perfect themselves in wisdom are called the twice-born, for by wisdom man is given a new birth. He departs from an old life with its uncertainties and limitations into a new, illumined existence. Pythagoras refers to the philosopher as "the deathless soul." The world we live in today is ruled by fear—fear of life and fear of death. Wisdom alone can overcome fear. Love rules the sphere of the wise and those who have learned to love life in its deepest and most mystical sense have escaped from bondage to fear and dwell in peace with all things.

This letter is, by necessity, an introductory. Next month we shall begin the outline of first principles with a discussion of the departments of metaphysics, and a summary of metaphysical teachings concerning the Supreme Source and development of the universe and man. I have been frequently requested to give in written form my own philosophy of life, and as far as possible, I shall do this through these letters, setting forth my own belief and understanding of the whole field of spiritual and metaphysical thought.

May I take this opportunity of thanking you for the interest and support which you have shown in my work and hope that these letters will form a new bond of friendship between us. If you have friends who are interested in these subjects, or who might be led to such an interest through these letters, may we suggest that you enroll these friends to receive the letters, thus helping to spread a doctrine of enlightenment which we feel sure will enrich their lives.

Yours sincerely,

Manly P. Hall

944 West 20th Street.
Los Angeles, Calif.

JUNE 1, 1934

Dear Friend,

In last month's letter, I defined philosophy as the science of essential wisdom and briefly outlined its seven parts. METAPHYSICS is the first branch of philosophy and therefore our lesson for this month will be devoted to Metaphysics.

The term Metaphysics is derived from two Greek words meaning "after physics," or "beyond those things which pertain to external nature." The generally accepted definitions of the term are derived from Aristotle, the

> AN EARLY PAGAN PRAYER "May I be no man's enemy, and may I be the friend of that which is Eternal and Abides. May I never quarrel with those nearest to me; and if I do, may I be reconciled quickly. May I never devise evil against any man; if any devise evil against me, may I escape uninjured and without the need of hurting him. May I love, seek, and attain that which is good. May I wish for all men's happiness and envy none. May I never rejoice in the ill-fortune of one who has wronged me—When I have done or said what is wrong, may I never wait for the rebuke of others, but always rebuke myself until I make amends.—May I win no victory that harms either me or my opponent—May I reconcile friends who are wroth with one another. May I, to the extent of my powers, give all needful help to my friend in danger. When visiting those in grief may I be able by gentle and healing words to soften their pain—May I respect myself—May I always keep tame that which rages within me—May I accustom myself to be gentle, and never be angry with people because of circumstances. May I never discuss who is wicked and what wicked things he has done, but know good men and follow in their footsteps."
>
> - Eusebius, an Ionic Platonist

first author to prepare a lengthy treatise under this name. Aristotle uses the term METAPHYSICS at one time as synonymous with wisdom and at another time as synonymous with theology. He also calls it the "first philosophy."

Broadly speaking, existence is divisible into two primary states, which Albertus Magnus termed "physical and transphysical." The study of the visible universe is called PHYSICS and the study of the invisible universe is called METAPHYSICS. To philosophers, all visible effects are suspended from, or supported by, invisible causes and Metaphysics is therefore that branch of learning which seeks to discover and understand the unseen Causes at work behind visible nature. Metaphysics then includes the following departments of learning:

1—The nature of Being.

2—The nature of God.

3—The nature of Knowledge.

4—The nature of Truth.

5—The nature of Energy.

6—The nature of Creation.

7—The nature of divine and human relationships.

The purpose of Metaphysics is to lead the mind from the consideration of forms and bodies to an understanding of the principles which animate these forms and bodies. The intellect which has discovered the divine essence in all things has the metaphysical viewpoint. In order that you may have a wording knowledge of philosophical fundamentals it is first necessary to lay a metaphysical foundation, that is a foundation in superphysical principles. Visible nature is but a small part of existence. Although we are limited to visible nature in our present state, we can never live intelligently or thinly accurately until we have some understanding of that larger world which extends beyond the physical shell of our environment.

According to Metaphysics, BEING is an eternal unchanging Principle and is denominated the First Cause. Pythagoras defines God as an immeasurable and inconceivable Being whose soul is composed of the substance of truth and whose body is composed of the substance of light. Being is also termed ESSENCE and EXISTENCE, every effort being made to discover a term appropriately impersonal with which to designate this eternal energy. The modes or aspects of Being are termed Beings of which there are three kinds. The first kind of Being is called the UNMOVED and is God. The second kind of Being is called the SELF-MOVING or the gods, chief of which are the Intelligences of the celestial bodies. The third kind of Being is called the MOVED and includes all bodies and forms to which life is imparted by spirit, soul or mind,—the chief of such creatures is man.

Maximus Tyrius thus sums up the matter: "There is one God, the king and father of all things, and many gods, sons of God, ruling in conjunction with Him." Thus, Metaphysics teaches us that God, is not a personality but rather that Divine Life upon which all things subsist and that this One Life manifests attributes which are also divine principles. These attributes are called the gods. These second gods are the agencies by which all physical life is supported. When Maximus Tyrius refers to the "risings and settings of the gods" he is referring to the ascending and descending of the stars and constellations which were regarded by the philosophers as the bodies of the secondary deities who move constantly in great orbits about the Throne of their Eternal Father.

That we may more fully understand the metaphysical approach to the mystery of First Cause, let us examine some of the old fragments which have descended to us from the great metaphysical institutions of the ancients. The monuments of the Egyptians are richly ornamented with lofty sentiments concerning Being and God. In the shrine of Nephi's at Sais, Being is denominated as: "All that was, is, and shall be." At Thebes, Ammon, the Father of the gods, is called "The Concealed Spirit which was from the beginning." In the Louvre papyrus, Being is described as "Goodness itself, Lord of time, who conductest eternity; and Akhnaton adores the Creator as "Beauty which, is Life."

The Greeks thus reasoned upon this Divine Mystery: According to Pythagoras, the Eternal Principle is Number and Harmony infinitely diffused. Thales had several definitions. "Being." he said, "is that which has neither beginning nor end, and is older than Time. All things are full of God. The mind of the universe is God." Xenophanes, lifting his eyes to the heavens, exclaims: "Words fail. The One is God." He further declared that the Infinite resembles mortals neither in form nor in thought but abides eternally, moving not at all, but causing all things to move. Aristotle defines the First Principle as eternal and perfect, without parts and passions, indivisible and unchanging, adding: "Bliss is the Self-activity of God."

The belief in an eternally-existing Principle, termed variously the One, the Beautiful and the Good, is the absolute foundation of Metaphysics. This Principle is termed in the Mahabharata "the Root Undying whence has sprung whatever is."

Thus, all great mystical theologies are primarily monotheistic—worshipping one supreme Principle—yet as this One Principle has produced out of Itself the immeasurable diversity which is perceptible in nature, the philosophers considered it appropriate to regard the attributes of First Cause as also divine. From this practice arose polytheism.

It is interesting to digress here for a moment and fix the meanings of certain terms. The votaries of the various religious systems of the world are divided into three classes. The first class is called CHRISTIAN, the second PAGAN, and the third HEATHEN. The term Christian is stretched to include both Jews and Mohammedans, as these three share the same original religious inspiration. The word PAGAN is defined by the dictionary as one who worships false gods. The definition later adds that a pagan is a heathen and that a heathen is one who does not belong to the Christian, Mohammedan or Jewish sects. Modern reason demands that we should understand the terms pagan and heathen in their true light. The term pagan is now generally bestowed upon all philosophic nations, Plato and Aristotle were pagans, but THEY DID NOT WORSHIP FALSE GODS. Truly speaking, a pagan is one who refuses to accept credal limitations of the Divine Essence. Pythagoras was a pagan because he was initiated into fourteen great world religions and permitted no sectarian boundaries to prejudice his mind concerning the universality of truth. The term HEATHEN implies false belief, ignorance of the nature of God, and polytheism. This term also Is applied to members of any religion other than Christian, Mohammedan and Jewish. The Hindus, for example, are termed heathens. First, because their pantheon is regarded as idolatrous by Christendom; second, because their definition of God differs from the Biblical definition; and lastly, because they are polytheistic.

It follows from these definitions that all philosophers are, to some degree pagans and heathens. Pagans because they respect no man-made religious limitation, and heathens because they realize that the one God controls Its creation through an elaborate polytheism—a vast order of secondary gods. Nor do the philosophers believe that these premises in any way conflict with the essential principles of the original Christian revelation.

If you are to become a truly enlightened metaphysician, you must be prepared to accept the presence of God in every element of nature and in every aspect of existence. Like the pagans of old, you must conceive the universe as full of Intelligent Principles. The old Jews bestowed upon the Creating Principle ten Ineffable Names by which Its qualities might be made known to the wise. One of these names was AL SHADDAI which means the LORD OF HOSTS. Thus, while divinity in its absolute essence is One and indivisible, man is not permitted to perceive Being in this absolute state. To mortal perception the Creating Power must alt ways be the Lord of Hosts. This simply means that Deity is so immersed in Its creating processes that we perceive not Its unity but Its absolute diversity. Yet as surely as it is appropriate to worship Its unity, so it is also appropriate to reverence Its diversity. If men build temples to the attributes of Deity, this is not necessarily because they are unaware of the essential unity which lies behind these attributes.

As metaphysicians, it is our philosophic privilege to worship and seek to understand the Lord of Hosts. We must sense the Creator as an innumerable army of Intelligent Building Agencies. Space is filled with the individualized aspects of divinity. The suns, moons and stars which populate the firmament are divine Beings, radiant Sons of the Infinite.

As surely as space is resplendent with the Heavenly Host, so surely "the earth is full of gods." By this statement, the pagan initiates inferred that men also are heavenly beings. Man himself is part of the divine host of gods, and all creatures, great and small, share divinity in common. One of the old Greek masters always addressed his prayer to the God who dwelt "in the heaven and in the heart."

We all desire to achieve security—spiritual, mental and physical. We know that security is conferred only by wisdom and only a wise man can rise above the ills the flesh is heir to. Heraclitus of Ephesus said: "Character is fate." This is probably one of the most significant statements ever uttered by man. Our destiny is measured by what we are. If we would come to a good end, we must possess a character which justifies that end. Character is made up of several factors. Chief of these is our philosophical perspective. We live upon the level of our thoughts and ideals.

If we are to elevate ourselves to a philosophical level, our first lesson is to seek to understand, at least in part, the origin of the universe and our own place therein, and to sense the sublimity of the divine plan. Contemplation of the transcendent beauties of this mystical theology will elevate our minds above those narrow and unworthy concepts which bind us to an ignoble state. It will give us a spiritual perspective by which we can live more usefully, happily, intelligently, and completely. We cannot consider lightly or as merely speculative the old metaphysical philosophies, for what can be more practical or more useful than a discipline which directs our attention to the nobler aspects of life and invites us into a mystical communion with that Eternal Spirit which dwells in the furthermost and the innermost?

In next month's letter, we shall continue our study of Metaphysics, dealing particularly with the Nature of Knowledge and the Nature of Truth.

Yours sincerely,

Manly P. Hall

944 West 20th Street,
Los Angeles, Calif.

THOUGHTS FROM A PHILOSOPHER'S SCRAPBOOK

"Chemistry reveals, for example, that a man weighing 150 pounds will contain approximately 3500 cubic feet of gas—oxygen, hydrogen and nitrogen—in his constitution, which at 80 cents per thousand cubic feet would be worth $2.80 for illuminating purposes. He also contains all the necessary fats to make a 5-pound candle, and thus, together with his 3500 cubic feet of gases, he possesses considerable illuminating possibilities. His system contains 22 pounds and 10 ounces of carbon, or enough to make 780 dozen, or 9360 lead pencils. There are about 50 grains of iron in his blood and the rest of the body would supply enough of this metal to make one spike large enough to hold his weight. A healthy man contains 54 ounces of phosphorus. This deadly poison would make 800,000 matches, or enough poison to kill 500 persons. This, with two ounces of lime, makes the stiff bones and brains. No difference how sour a man looks, he contains about 60 lumps of sugar of the ordinary cubical dimensions, and to make the seasoning complete, there are 20 spoonful's of salt. If a man were distilled into water, he would make about 38 quarts, or more than half his entire weight. He also contains a great deal of starch, chloride of potash, magnesium, sulfur and hydrochloric acid in his wonderful human system."

—From a newspaper clipping.

*****

Ptolemy Philopater, king of Egypt, built a ship 420 feet in length and 78 feet in height from the bottom to the upper deck. It had four hundred banks or seats of rowers, four hundred mariners, and four thousand rowers, and on the decks, it could contain three thousand soldiers. There were also gardens and orchards on top of it, as Plutarch relates in the life of Demetrius.

*****

"On December 5, 1664, a vessel crossing the Menal strait with eighty-one passengers on board encountered a terrific gale and foundered. The only man who escaped death was Hugh Williams. More than a hundred years later, on December 5, 1780, another vessel with a large number of passengers sank in the same circumstances and in the same place. All the passengers were drowned, except one, again a Hugh Williams. Again, on December 5, 1820, a boat laden with thirty people sank into the same spot. The sole survivor once more was a Hugh Williams.—From Star of the Magi

*****

"If intense suffering comes, turn away your mind and conquer the pain by the 'sweetness' of memory. There are in every man's life moments of intense beauty and delight; if he has strength of mind, he will call them back to him at will and live in the blessedness of the past, not in the mere agony of the moment."—Epicuras

JULY 1, 1934

Dear Friend,

Aristotle opens his celebrated treatise ON METAPHYSICS with the statement: "All men naturally desire to know." The 3rd and 4th branches of Metaphysics are concerned with the substance and nature of KNOWLEDGE and the relationship between things known and that abstract state of knowing which we term TRUTH.

In his famous work THE NEW ATLANTIS, Sir Francis Bacon describes a philosophic empire, ruled over by enlightened men, which is some day to be established upon the earth. In the midst of this empire is the City of Wisdom, and in the midst of this city, a university of the arts and sciences named SOLOMON'S HOUSE. The master of this House thus describes the true purpose of knowledge: "The end of our foundation is the knowledge of Causes, and the secret motions of things; and the enlarging of the bounds of human empire, to the effecting of all things possible."

Lord Bacon was the father of modern science, and his definition of knowledge reveals a clear perception of spiritual values. He tells us that the end of all science is the knowledge of causes, that we may perceive not only things themselves but the reasons for them. Our quest for reasons must inevitably lead us to philosophy, especially that branch which we call Metaphysics. The causes and reasons behind all natural phenomena exist in the invisible and subjective part of nature—the divine part. It is here that we must search for them if we are to become truly wise.

Knowledge enlarges the bounds of human empire because it is an occult maxim that man's own nature extends to the circumference of his understanding. As we grow in knowledge, we truly enlarge ourselves, becoming, in fact, part of everything that we know. We flow outward along the radiations of our appreciation until at last, according to the old Mysteries, we know everything and become a part of everything.

Lord Bacon describes the reward which knowledge bestows by his statement that through the enlargement of it, we are finally able to accomplish all things that are possible.

> THE PRAYER OF SOCRATES
>
> "Beloved Pan, and all ye diviner Ones about this place, grant that I may be good in the inner nature, and that what I have of external things may be accordant with those within. May I deem the wise man truly rich, and let me have only such an amount of material wealth as a provident man may possess and wisely use."

By "possible" he means consistent with the laws of being. Among possible things must be included the final perfection of man himself and the releasing through his organisms all of the spiritual, intellectual and physical powers which are latent within him. The word knowledge has several meanings, measured by the understanding of the individual who uses it.

The word knowledge may either infer a broad spiritual perception or it may signify little more than accumulated prejudices. For the sake of definition, we may say that knowledge may be either formal or relative. Formal or absolute knowledge exists only in the Divine Nature itself and is alone discoverable by the inner perceptions of an enlightened soul. This is because the soul itself, being part of the Divine Nature, partakes subjectively of divine knowledge. Relative knowledge is based on tradition, observation and experimentation and is concerned chiefly with the elements and conditions of the temporal state. All so-called scientific knowledge, under our present system of education, must be relative. All knowledge derived from books must be relative, for relative knowledge comes from without—absolute knowledge from within.

We must now distinguish between KNOWLEDGE and TRUTH, for, since the confusion of tongues, words have lost caste. Truth is an inclusive term, while knowledge suggests a fragmentary condition. Thus, we say, "there are many forms of knowledge," as for example the seven liberal arts and sciences, but philosophically speaking, we can never say there are many forms of truth, for truth infers a fundamental, unchanging, unconditioned reality—the fact per se. One of the old philosophers has said that truth is a divine light, invisible to mortal eyes, but all-penetrating. Matter is a prism.

The light of truth, striking this prism, breaks into a spectrum—a spectrum of intellectual colors. These colors considered separately are the departments of knowledge. Thus, knowledge is truth conditioned and broken up, but all real knowledge contains within it some element of truth. Some part of the whole is in all of the parts, even as some part of God is in every part of nature.

Man is capable of containing knowledge or of accumulating it, storing up in himself facts out of experience. But no man is capable of containing truth in himself, of collecting it or storing it up. To create a definition:

The individual absorbs knowledge, but Truth absorbs the individual.

The alchemists called truth Mercury because it was a common solvent which bound all things together. It recognizes no boundaries or divisions, but penetrates all existence so universally that it can never be captured or limited by any organism.

The rational principle in man ascends by a seven runged-ladder from the darkness of its material condition to the luminance of its spiritual state. Speaking in terms of knowledge, the seven rungs of this ladder represent seven sequential steps in the apprehension of fact. The lowest step is perception, which is possessed by even the most primitive types who abide in the unquestioned acceptance of things seen. From perception, the intellect rises to examination, from examination to reflection. What we call education today is merely the racial inheritance of things seen, examined, and reflected upon. From reflection, the reasoning part (commonly termed the mind) rises to knowledge, which is a synthesis of the three former processes. From knowledge, it rises to understanding; from understanding to wisdom; and from wisdom, it ascends finally to Truth.

Knowledge, being the 4th step in the unfoldment of reason, occupies a middle distance between the three inferior and the three superior parts. It therefore was regarded by the ancient philosophers as symbolical of the Sun which, in the old geocentric systems of astrology, moved upon the 4th orbit of the world, dividing the planetary family into three inferior and three superior bodies. According to the same doctrine, knowledge was peculiarly associated with man in that the human creation occupied the 4th round of the creative process.

Knowledge, like man, then, occupies a neutral position between the inferior and superior worlds. Below knowledge lies instinct and the physical perceptions. Above knowledge rises intuition and the spiritual perceptions. Thus, knowledge unites the two worlds—the divine and the animal. Conversely, knowledge also divides them.

Knowledge is an instrument by the possession and proper use of which an enlightened individual can come gradually to perceive the invisible forces at work behind the visible elements of life. Knowledge, illumined by spiritual purpose, lifts the soul to understanding. Knowledge, unillumined and undirected, depresses the soul into a sphere of criticism and skepticism, an evil state into which, alas, most of our educational institutions have fallen.

In the old Mystery dramas, disciples wandering in the chambers of initiation (the sphere of experience) were always accompanied by an ancient man, sometimes called "the kindly or venerable guide." This aged person—Gurnemanz in the opera of Parsifal; Merlin in the Arthurian Cycle, etc.—represents the spiritual emotion of veneration. This power is represented as aged and kindly because it is born of suffering and experience and has travelled long on the road of life. No man who approaches the mysteries of nature without veneration can find his way through the tortuous passage-ways of scientific uncertainties.

The uninformed man fears life, the informed man comes to respect life, but only the wise man, enriched with understanding, loves and venerates life. Thus, perception, examination and reflection may lead to misgivings; knowledge may impart a certain sense of security; but understanding, wisdom and truth bestow illumined appreciation of the sublimity of existence.

Let us define understanding that we may perceive in what it differs from knowledge. To borrow a simile from the Lohar, one of the ancient cabbalists said: All things are invested with outer garments which we term bodies or forms and which are analogous to the clothing worn by man. To judge of any living thing by its form alone is equal to judging a man by his clothes alone. Knowledge permits us to examine the clothing of things but may bestow no appreciation of that which is beneath the garments. Knowledge, therefore, will teach us to say: This is a rock, this is a plant, this is a man. But this is only equal to saying: This is a hat, these are shoes that is a coat. A man is not merely his hat, coat or shoes, though to the uninformed he may appear identical to them. Nor is nature rock, plant or man. These are but words for forms. An educated man may know the proper names for these forms, thus possessing a certain form of knowledge, yet, lacking the ability to discover that which is hidden within these garments, he lacks understanding and his knowledge profits him nothing. Beneath all garments are bodies very different from the garments that conceal them. Within these bodies are souls and these souls, in turn conceal principles of intellect and sense. Behind intellect and sense is spirit. He who understands this achieves wisdom; he who is ignorant of this is unworthy to be termed learned, for learning without wisdom can never achieve to Truth.

Understanding implies what Paracelsus terms "sympathy." Not the superficial emotion to which we commonly apply that term, but rather a condition of rapprochement, attunement, or at-one-ment. Understanding removes the barriers of separateness which divide one living thing from another. This results in what is termed the "mystical communion," for communion is "union in consciousness."

From understanding, therefore, we ascend to wisdom. Wisdom is a condition of consciousness rather than an attitude of mind. Wisdom is that state of being in which an individual finds himself when realization has tinctured and transmuted all attitudes and opinions. A wise man is one who has experienced wisdom, wisdom in this sense being a mystical experience. Our common term "enthusiasm" meant to the ancients "wisdom!" It is derived from the Greek word "entheos"—in God. To the old mystics, it was the ecstatic condition of conscious—ness—attunement with the great mystery of life. As Jacob Boehme, the illumined shoemaker, would have expressed if. It is the plant of the human soul bursting into flower in God.

This leads us naturally to Pilate's eternal question—What is Truth? Again, we must create a definition: Truth is God as fact. In other words, Deity is the consummation of every condition and extension of energy conceivable by man. Thus, God, in terms of time or extension, is Eternity. God, in terms of emotion, is divine love. God, in terms of morality, is absolute virtue; and God, in terms of fact, is absolute Truth. To know Truth, therefore, one must know God and to know God man must have discovered divinity in all of its manifestations and have become one with that divinity.

The search for Truth is life. The realization of Truth is illumination. The practice of Truth is virtue. Truth is the Hermetic medicine, the universal panacea, the balm of Gilead which cures all of the diseases which are caused by ignorance.

It is not given to man that in his present undeveloped condition that he shall be fully possessed by Truth. He must achieve this ultimate good by that pilgrimage, which is called evolution. In India, holy men perform symbolic pilgrimages, visiting in a prescribed sequence the shrines of the various divinities that represent the various aspects of knowledge. The Greek philosopher Cebes designed a curious table or tablet which depicts the progress of the human soul. Man is depicted as ascending a mountain by a circuitous path. The top of the mountain is concealed by clouds and, upon the very peak, invisible to the world below, is a glorious temple. This is the temple of wisdom and within it are luminous figures representing enlightened and perfected souls. In some old drawings, the roof of this temple is supported by three columns. These columns are Integrity, Loyalty and Appreciation, according to the old Mysteries. These three columns must uphold the temple of philosophy. In the heavens above, the temple itself is an immense radiant light, the only symbol by which absolute Truth may be appropriately represented.

We are all striving to ascend the mountain of knowledge. Its circuitous path, beset with many dangers and difficulties, represents the daily life of the individual. If we possess sufficient fortitude and sincerity, we shall finally reach the temple concealed by clouds.

Michael Maier, the Rosicrucian adept, wrote that the House of the Holy Spirit, the most secret temple of the Rose Cross, was upon the crest of a mighty mountain, higher even than Olympus. He also explained that this House is always concealed by clouds so that the profane and unworthy may not be able to discover it. A narrow path leads through the dense mist, however, and to those who are worthy, the path is revealed.

It is appropriate that wisdom should be shown as seated upon the highest parts of the world. By highest is meant the most spiritual and refined part. The prophet exclaims: "I will lift up mine eyes unto the hills, from whence cometh my help." The hearts of enlightened men are the high places of the earth. In the hearts of those who love Truth the gods dwell together.

Metaphysics not only describes the creation of the world, but it also reveals the mystical anatomy of God. In the midst of the great body of the Eternal One is the luminous Heart, the everlasting House, the Universal Temple. Those who are seeking for Truth are seeking the heart of God and those who discover Truth and who are possessed by it are one with the heart of God.

Yours sincerely,

Manly P. Hall

THOUGHTS FROM A PHILOSOPHER'S SCRAPBOOK

The most important sale of occult books in the last hundred years took place In London recently. On April 16th, 17th, and 18th, the firm of Sotheby and Company auctioned off the library of Mr. Lionel Hauser, a prominent member of the Theosophical Society of France. The collection included many rare books and manuscripts dealing with alchemy, cabbalism, and Rosicrucianism. Among the manuscripts was a book of ceremonial magic, written in cipher, on velum, prepared by the celebrated adept, Comte de St. Germain, for one of his disciples. Through the generosity of a friend, Mr. Hall has become the possessor of this book, which he has decoded and will publish in the near future.

AUGUST 1, 1934

Dear Friend,

Few authentic fragments have descended to us of the words of Pythagoras. Justin Martyr has preserved the following little-known quotation from the Samian Sage:

"God is one. He is not, as some thinly, without the world, but within it, and entire in its entirety. Heswers and performances, the origin of all things, the Light of Heaven, the Father, the Intelligence, the Soul of all beings, the Mover of all spheres."

The fifth and sixth departments of Metaphysics deal particularly with God as the "Mover of all spheres," the last attribute bestowed upon Deity by Pythagoras in the above definition. Therefore, this lesson will be devoted to the nature of Energy and the nature of Creation, or the manifestation of Energy in worlds.

Modern science, in its effort to escape from the overshadowing influence of theology, has built a barrier of terminology between itself and the old mystical teachings. Although it has coined new words for old ideas, it has not been able, in any essential particular, to change the substance of these ideas; nor has science been able to substitute for the ancient theologies any more adequate explanation of universal Cause, purpose or destiny. Thus, a scientist may reject the Christian trinity of Father, Son and Holy Ghost as imaginary personalities, yet in the face of this refection he postulates consciousness, intelligence and force as the foundations of existence, thus remaining a true trinitarian, consoling his prejudice with words alone.

The ancient philosophers affirmed the material universe to be suspended from the third aspect of the Divine Nature. This third aspect they denominated the Demiurges, the Cosmocratore, the Artificer, the Feather of the Builders. The Greeks called him Zeus, and the Latins Jupiter. Thus, platonically speaking, the material universe is Deity in the aspect of Energy or action.

The modern scholar has relegated Jupiter-Pan (the god of unfolding nature) to the limbo, substituting therefor the neutral term "energy."

> This also we humbly beg, that Human Things may not prejudice such as are Divine, neither that from the unlocking of the Gates of Sense and the kindling of a greater Natural Light, anything of credulity or intellectual night may arise in our minds toward Divine Mysteries.—Sir Francis Bacon

The principle remains unchanged. We have gained nothing by the new word, in fact, we have lost. Energy as Zeus was not only a subject for study but also one for veneration. The divine quality which the ancient theologists discovered in all parts of nature has been destroyed by the modern attitude towards learning. Thus, energy is God with its divinity and intelligence left out and only its force remaining. The first step in the rescuing of the metaphysical tradition is, therefore, the reestablishment of the divine principle in substance and behind activity. Energy is now defined as inherent power, whereas in ancient times it was defined as inherent Divinity. Energy is further defined as a capacity for acting, thus it is the Mover of the Orphics. Energy is the root of force, even as it is the support of phenomenal life. A study of energy involves two issues, its origin and its use. The universe is, composed of the substance of Being, is established by and in the substance of Wisdom, and is supported by and in the substance of Force. Thus, energy is the foundation of the whole material universe, the pedestal which upholds the world. In India, it is indeed Vishnu who, in the form of the strong animal, the boar, elevates creation upon his tusks.

In the Cabala, the Tree of Life consists of three major trunks from which emanate numerous branches. These trunks are called Wisdom, Strength and Beauty and by them the creation is maintained. It is from these three trunks that Christendom has derived its triad of moral virtues—faith, hope and charity. Faith is the highest form of wisdom, hope is the noblest aspect of strength, and charity is moral beauty. The Pythagoreans also had a triad of Being, Life and Light which supported their world order. To them, the world issued from the principle of Light, for which reason Pythagoras declared the body of God to be composed of light. Light is the most perfect of all forms, for in it the energy principle is the least obscured by material elements. We find reference to this thought in the first chapter of John: "In the beginning was the Word." By the Word, Logos, or Fiat, is inferred Deity in its attribute of energy or force. John then says of God: "In Him was life; and the life was the light of man!" Thus, the gospel establishes the Pythagorean foundation—God or Being, life and light. Though science may involve the issue by developing an elaborate terminology by which the simple truths become obscured by phraseology, the spiritual foundations of the world remain unmoved. The well-being of each individual depends upon his ability to rescue spiritual values from their present obscuration and to live in accordance with these values.

The ancients, in explaining the mystery of what we call energy, which to them was an emanation from divine Beings, classified these forces under several headings. There is first intellectual energy which emanates from the Zodiac and of which the body of Zeus, or the world-God, was formed. Intellectual energy was divided by Plato into two aspects, termed intelligible and intellectual. Intelligible intellect was the energy of pure knowing—knowing being higher than thinking, for knowing comes from within and thinking which is intellectual intellect, arises from external stimulus.

Second, there is psychical energy which emanates from the planets. This energy is both compound and complex, for in every evidence of it there is an admixture of the several qualities of the planetary bodies. This energy is moral and sensory. From it arises the impulsive and appetitive parts.

The third is vital energy, which originates from the Sun and forms, so to speak, a common nutrition by which all physical organisms are supported. This energy is truly the food of the material world, and all so-called nourishment arises from the presence of this nutritive energy in various foodstuffs. Around this principle, modern scientists have built the vitamin theory.

The fourth is corruptive energy, originating from the Moon and bringing the corrosive, disintegrative principle of decay with it. The corruptive energy is necessary to prevent a stagnation of vital currents. Corruption preserves the circulation of energy by destroying organisms in which this energy has been collected and locked. The fifth and last energy is seminal energy which arises from the earth itself and has, as its special province, the perpetuation of fertility. Without this special aspect of energy, the propagative principle would fail, even as without solar energy the nutritive power would cease.

Thus, by philosophy, we come to know that we live, move and have our being in a sea of divine energy, supported by the Infinite Wisdom, and nourished by the Infinite Life. Energy as capacity or capability is also an opportunity. As the infinite opportunity to do, it is by reflex the opportunity to be or to accomplish through action. Energy is that "magical agent" of the old transcendentalists by the proper use of which we build character and through the perversion of which we destroy ourselves and our world. Virtue and vice are manifestations of our capacity for action. No man thinks, feels or moves of himself but because of God (energy) within him. Every thought, emotion and action is a sacred mystery and not a meaningless accident, as materialists would have us think. Wisdom arises out of the right use of mental energy; virtue out of the right use of emotional energy; and health out of the balance and integrity of physical energy. Life is a spiritual adventure in the use of divine forces and energies. He who uses them well lives well and is himself in a state of well-being.

From the study of energy, we naturally come to the nature of creation, for creation as a process is energy directed towards the formative processes. Creation as a condition is the manifested universe arising from the chemistry of energy and supported thereby.

As we look, about us at the multitude of forms which exist together in what we call the world, it is sometimes difficult for us to perceive the causes which brought these forms into being. We are bewildered by diversity, yet without some understanding of the reason for things as they are, we cannot intelligently cooperate with the plan of life. What we commonly call creation is, philosophically speaking, formation. It is not really something coming out of nothing, but rather forms growing from their seeds. Growth is energy unfolding through organisms. Things do not grow—energy unfolds in them. As the old theologians said, growth is God unfolding in his creations. Energy, moving from within outward, causes expansion. Expansion requires organization to support it. Organization, in turn becomes a nucleus for further expansion. In the physical world, this expansion, organization, expansion, etc. is accompanied by a certain physical increase. Upon the whole process we bestow the term growth. All things grow first in their internal parts, and their external parts merely increase to accommodate this internal expansion.

Man is constantly growing. For millions of years, he has been evolving his present organism to meet the needs of the unfolding internal principle. Every organ and member of his physical body was the product of a desperate necessity for that organ and member. Every new faculty or soul power which man develops results in some modification and improvement in his physical structure. The human fingers are the product of millions of years of impulse. As time goes on, the body of man will be still more greatly refined, new parts and members will be added, and the spiritual capacities will be markedly increased. These changes will bear witness to the eternal creative principle, to the action of which, according to Plato, there is no beginning, end, or limitation. Energy and the creative impulse, working in partnership together, are the Builders of the worlds and their creatures. In space, vast creative or formative processes are constantly going on. In the soul of man, similar processes are continuously in action. The infinite potentiality for progress which is inherent in every atom of being is evident in what the ancients termed the "growing up of space."

Man, in the small sphere of his own existence, is not only part of the growing whole; he has evolved to the place where he is capable of being a conscious agent, cooperating voluntarily with the divine order. He is capable of directing and using energy; he is capable of a mental, emotional and physical creative expression. What we term civilization, in its more refined aspects, is evidence to the creative impulse in man. The arts and sciences are avenues of expression. It is within the power of the intelligent man and woman to contribute a truly creative impulse to society. The old Mystery Schools taught that true religion consisted of the right use of energy and opportunity; of realizing that the life which supports us is a sacred and spiritual force, the reverent use of which was regarded as a spiritual virtue. The misuse of energy and the inadequate or destructive use of the Divine Agent indicates an immature spiritual viewpoint. The purpose of energy is to create, preserve, and beautify. Its proper use increases the amount of manifested good. The philosopher, realizing the energies of life to be the very bodies and souls of the gods, endeavors to use every element of his living to produce some permanent and constructive effect. The wasting of energy, its misuse or abuse, is a sacrilege of which no wise man wishes to be guilty.

By destroying the moral values of action and reducing the whole universal plan to a mechanistic program, science destroys the spiritual equation in action. Deprived in this way of its noblest part, action loses its virtue and becomes a contributing cause of the world's woe. No one who sincerely understands the divine factors in life can be guilty of those evil doings by which our civilization is being destroyed. Energy is necessary to activate any motion, be it constructive or destructive. Creation comes into being through activated motion. Our ambitions, hopes, desires, etc. are the basis of the institutions which we upbuild. Life is a constant and continual sacrament. We live off of the blood of the gods and because our whole sustenance is divine, our lives should also be divinely inspired and we should live a code of action worthy of the spiritual life by which this code is supported.

Yours sincerely,

Manly P. Hall

944 West 20th Street.
Los Angeles, Calif.

THOUGHTS FROM A PHILOSOPHER'S SCRAPBOOK

Croesus, King of Lydia, is the richest man mentioned in ancient history. But wealth, like all of life's material factors, is relative and illusionary. The wealth of Croesus has been estimated about $8,500,000 in landed estates. There are several fortunes in the world today which are in excess of $1,000,000,000. If he lived today, Croesus would be a man of only "medium circumstances", yet he remains the personification of wealth.

*****

The first Christian hymn was written by the pagan emperor Hadrian. The hymn starts with the words, "Vital spark of heavenly flame." Hadrian was a persecutor of the Christians, but otherwise a fust and enlightened ruler.

*****

The so-called essential doctrines of the Christian Church were established by a series of Councils. These Councils actually legislated the divinity of Christ.

The First Council, at Nice, in 325, defended the divinity of Christ against the Arians who denied this divinity.

The Second Council, at Constantinople, in 381, opposed the Apollinarians, who denied that Christ was a human being.

The Third Council, at Ephesus, in 431, confuted the arguments of the Nestorians, who affirmed that in Christ are two persons, one human and the other divine.

The Fourth Council, at Chalcedon, in 451, confuted the heresy of the Eutychians, who maintained that in Christ the human and Divine natures were utterly mingled into one identity.

A considerable part of the ancient Church took no part in these Councils, but all Christendom has been influenced by their decisions.

*****

A man will do strange things in the hope that future ages will remember him. A Greek philosopher jumped into the crater of a volcano so that his body might be entirely destroyed and his disciples would believe that he had ascended to heaven. Herostratus burned the Temple of Diana at Ephesus because he believed that history would never forget the name of the man who committed so terrible an act. Hakim Ben Allah, the Veiled Prophet of Khorasan, ended his life by casting himself into a great vat filled with burning acid in the hope that future members of his sect might be able to say that he had disappeared, leaving no mortal part.

SEPTEMBER 1, 1934

Dear Friend,

The seventh and last department of Metaphysics deals with the Nature of Divine and Human Relationships. The term theological is generally applied to that branch of metaphysics which attempts to coordinate spiritual and physical laws.

The visible universe is regarded by mystical philosophers as the shadow or reflection in matter of the invisible spiritual universe. In the ancient writings, the spiritual universe is termed the superior sphere, for in it abide the Principles of all things. The term "principles" in this case infers not only the essential substance or spiritual part of every nature but also the laws and patterns by which these spiritual parts exist and unfold themselves. The antithesis of spirit is matter, and the material universe therefore is regarded as a sort of ground or earth in which the spiritual principles are sown as seed and in which each grows up according to its own law. As the physical forms of plants grow upward towards the physical sun and unfold themselves in and by its energy, so the spiritual dispositions of all creatures expand towards the spiritual sun, are sustained in and by it, and come to their perfections in its effulgency.

The initiated philosophers, in harmony with this concept of divine order, classified all knowledge under two headings—sacred and profane. They defined sacred learning as primary knowledge, and profane learning as secondary knowledge. The term "primary knowledge" infers a knowledge founded upon the understanding of spiritual causes. Secondary knowledge infers the absence of the spiritual factor. Any system of thinking which ignores the divine foundation of life is said to be lacking in primary fact and is therefore secondary or profane.

Materialism is a comparatively modern invention of the human mind. Materialism not only ignores, but actually denies the metaphysical factor in thought and action. Antiquity was dedicated to its gods. The princes of the ancient states acknowledged their vassalage to that divine kingdom which extends throughout all space and is absolute in its dominion. The modern world acknowledges no authority beyond the petty despotisms which it sets up and circumscribes with its small vision and purpose. Man has exiled himself from the empire of space and is satisfied to live without wisdom and die without hope.

One of the primary functions of metaphysics is to incline the human reason towards an intelligent consideration of man's place in the divine plan. Metaphysics seeks to establish a closer harmony between divine will and human action. Metaphysics does not infer blind faith, or the unquestioned worship of unknown gods, but rather seeks to establish a rational sympathy between heaven and earth, a conscious and intelligent cooperation between man and the laws that govern him. The numerous evils which afflict the race, the crimes and disasters from which we suffer, are most of them traceable to the absence of the metaphysical factor in education and life.

We feel that a philosophical definition of heaven, as distinct from the modern theological concept thereof, may result in a better understanding of spiritual factors. Theologists, blinded by their jot and tittle creeds, have come to regard heaven as a place, distant and formal, populated by a spiritual genus, and ruled over by a capricious anthropomorphic deity. This celestial despotism exists nowhere except in the imagination of the unenlightened.

The heaven of the wise is Space itself—an immeasurable empire extending throughout the uttermost extremities of being. This empire of Universal Life, established upon the immovable foundations of existence, is populated by a myriad of principles—"luminous energies" as the ancients called them—"gods" as they were known to the pagans.

Heaven is the empire of truth and fact. He who abides in truth and, according to fact, abides in the celestial world, but he who lives in his opinions and conceits is exiled to the outer darkness. Hermes said that the law of analogy was the priceless key to divine mysteries. With the aid of this law the ancient philosophers explored the heavenly world, creating a divine science which they preserved in their temples, imparting its elements only to those whom they regarded as worthy of so noble a learning.

Though man springs like a plant from the earth and, like the dying plant, returns to it again, the ancients affirmed that his growth bore witness to a Divine Energy. It is not the body of man that grows, it is a life growing up within the body which causes the appearance of growth. Nor again, is death the dying of this life but rather its deflection from physical purpose. Man abides a little time in the conceit of matter and then, in the words of Homer, returns to his long-lost native land—the empire of spirit. How noble then is that philosophy by the possession of which the human being prepares himself for universal citizenship!

The mystery of divine and human relationships is preserved in the mystical literature of the Greeks under the fable of the wanderings of Ulysses. As a great part of metaphysical philosophy is derived from the theology of the Greeks, it is appropriate that we should have recourse to their mythologies for the keys to their spiritual wisdom. Homer, the greatest poet among the Greeks, is said to have been blind, but the esoteric traditions declare this blindness to have signified that Homer had been initiated into the Mysteries. His sight had been turned inward from external things so that he beheld no longer the material world but gazed into spiritual verities.

The Iliad and the Odyssey are masterpieces of mystical allegory. No other literary achievement approaches them in a wealth of symbolism. We would suggest that students of metaphysics familiarize themselves with these two works. With the exception of a short article by Thomas Taylor, which forms an appendix to his translation of Porphyry, no attempt has been made, as far as we are able to discover, to interpret the obscure symbolism of the Trojan War. The city of Troy, or more correctly, Ilion, was founded by Illus, the grandfather of Priam, the last King of Troy. The name Ilion is derived from the word "Illus," a term anciently used by the Greeks to signify mud, that is, primordial matter, mingled with the fluidic generative principle of life. Thus, the city of Ilion means the primitive ooze or slime from which all material bodies have their origins, and which even material science acknowledges to have been the source whence sprang the reptilian creations of the antediluvian world. The Iliad of Homer is therefore the mystical account of the descent of human souls (the Greeks) into the Illus or mud of generation.

In the Iliad the Greeks are referred to as foreigners, or strangers, to further indicate that they represented the spiritual principles in man which are indeed foreign to the material state wherein they are now placed. The Greeks anciently regarded themselves as of divine origin, and Homer makes use of this tradition to emphasize his point. The Trojans, on the other hand, are represented as at home in their own city, and as indigenous to the land in which they dwelt, whereas the Greeks came from a great distance in ships, over a vast ocean. According to Proclus, the Trojans represent the substances, energies and laws which are intrinsic to matter. The conquest of Troy by the Greeks therefore symbolizes that, in the beginning of the creative process, the irrational sphere or Chaos (Troy) was overcome or conquered by divinely enlightened reason (the Grecians).

The armies which the Greeks led against Troy were under the leadership of seven Heroes. These are the Creator-gods of the ancient cosmogony myths. We have parallels to them in the Ammonean Artificers of the Egyptians, and the Elohim of the Jews. They are the divinities who move upon the Deep or the Illus, conquering it and bringing it into a state of order, or, as Hesiod puts it, they brought Cosmos out of Chaos. The leader of the Greek armies was Agamemnon who represents the planet Jupiter, the Archimagus of the heavenly hosts, and his companion-generals are the remaining spheres of the ancient system. Menelaus, the husband of Helen, is the Moon, the source of the generative principle of which Helen is the symbol. The abduction of Helen by Paris is another form of the myth in which she is described as falling from the Moon in a silver egg.

Achilles, the most illustrious of the warriors in his golden armor, is the Sun, the St Michael of Christendom. Diomede, second only to Achilles in his glory, is Venus which is second only to the Sun in light. Ajax of gigantic strength and courage, but slow of mind, is Mars. Ulysses, famed for his strategy and his numerous eccentric journeyings, is Mercury, the swiftest and most erratic of the planets and patron of the intellect. Last of all, aged Nestor, the councilor and sage to whom all the generals turned for deep advice, is ancient Saturn the oldest and wisest of the gods.

Under the seven leaders or planets are the armies of souls—the Grecian host. These are life-waves coming into incarnation in the material world. They are the star-born mortals who acknowledge allegiance to their father-stars. After the Trojan War was over, each of these armies, under its proper leadership, returned by a different road to its own land. The various courses of these armies represent the many paths of evolution by which the waves of human souls return ultimately to their spiritual estate.

In the Odyssey we follow Ulysses, a heroic soul of the order of Mercury, along the adventurous course of evolution. He represents the human soul which, having descended into matter and established itself in the material sphere by honorable and heroic action, now seeks to improve and perfect its condition and return to its heavenly father and eternal kingdom. Ulysses therefore enters into the cycle of initiations—magnificently represented by his wanderings. This cycle is called "a sacred year" or the Twelve Months of the Gods. It is represented, as always, in the Mystery traditions, by the passage of the Sun through the twelve signs of the Zodiac. Thus, Ulysses performs his twelve labors of regeneration, becoming worthy in due time to be reestablished in his divine nature.

It is evident from the order of the "trials" or "tests" that the Odyssey in its present form dates from the time when the vernal equinox took place in the sign of Taurus, and, as Virgil says, "the bull of the year broke the annual egg with his horns!" The "adventures" of the Odyssey may therefore be arranged in the following order, according to the sacred year:

TAURUS: the adventure of the Lotophagi or the Lotus-eaters. Here Ulysses and his companions are tempted by the intoxicating pleasures of the appetites. They are invited to forget their spiritual aspirations and satisfy their souls with terrestrial luxuries. But Ulysses, under patronage of Minerva, the initiatrix, rescues his followers from the illusion and they press on to nobler action.

GEMINI: The adventure of the Cyclops, or the one-eyed giants. These are symbolical of the lower intellect with its lack of perspective. They are the primitive, mindless monsters of instinct and habit. Ulysses must overcome their irrational excesses which he does by driving a stake into the single eye by which he blinds the daemon and escapes back to his ships.

CANCER: The adventure of Aeolus, the god of the winds. The winds here represent the power of phantasy and imagination by the loosing of which the ship of life is blown from its course. This occurs when Ulysses is asleep and his companions (his instincts) are left without spiritual guidance.

LEO: The adventure of the Lestrigons. These are a race of giants that sink the ships of the Grecians, with the exception of one vessel upon which Ulysses escapes. Here, Leo's impulse to tyranny and ambition is represented as a race of immense destructive forces which terrorize the helpless.

VIRGO: The adventure with Circe, the enchantress. Circe changes her victims into swine even as Delilah, the Virgo of the Cabbalists, destroyed the strength of Samson. She is the illusion of materiality and the power of the senses. By the use of the sacred "moly" branch which was carried in the initiation ceremonials, Ulysses was able to overcome the enchantments of Circe and rescue his companions (impulses) from the spell of worldliness.

LIBRA: The adventure of the descent into the underworld. With Libra, the first half of the Zodiacal mystery is completed. The Sun descends into the underworld in the mystery of winter. In Hades Ulysses beholds the rewards of evil and receives instruction in the karmic justice of the gods.

SCORPIO: The adventure with the Sirens or temptresses. Here Ulysses and his companions fall under the spell of the carnal emotions. They are lured from their course by the magic song of the animal soul. Ulysses protects himself by lashing his body to the mast of his ship. The mast is principle or truth, and the ropes that tie him are self-control.

SAGITTARIUS: The adventure in judgment. This sign is the original Trojan horse containing within it the army of small stars by which the city of Troy is finally overcome. The wanderings of Ulysses consist of this intrepid mariner steering the course of his vessel safely between the rocks of Scylla and Charybdis. This represents the equilibrating of the mind in which the extremes of thought and action are balanced. All excess must be avoided by the wise.

CAPRICORN: The adventure of the Trinacrian Isle. Here while Ulysses is asleep (that is while the soul is obscured by material impulse) his comrades kill some of the sacred cattle of the Sun. This is the lesson in the sacredness of all life. Even as the dead skins of the cattle moved upon the ground, so evil deeds live on to convict us. Here also Calypso, the possessive instinct, is overcome.

AQUARIUS: The adventure of the Phaeacians. This represents the domain of reason and the Fortunate Isles. Here Ulysses sees Minerva disguised as a maiden with a vessel of water on her shoulder. Ulysses is tempted to dwell in the land of the wise and the happy, but he seeks a still higher god and continues on beyond any good which can be achieved in the material world.

PISCES: The adventure of the anger of Neptune. In this allegory Neptune represents the lord of the generating world, and when Ulysses attempts to ascend to the gods which are above, Neptune is depicted as attempting to prevent this escape by creating storms of material problems to deflect the divine adventurer from his purpose.

ARIES: In this cycle the end is achieved in the sign of Aries. Ulysses, disguised as a beggar, to signify that he has discarded all material attachments, has kindly come back to his own land. He is alone for all the attitudes and opinions (his companions while in the material state) have been lost upon the way. Ulysses reveals himself to his son Telemachus who represents truth in its divine and unconditioned state. Telemachus is the son of Ulysses, the rational soul, in union with Penelope, the personification of the Mystery School, or, as Homer indicates, divine philosophy. The suitors of Penelope who are attempting to steal away her husband's kingdom, represent the corruptions which have sought to destroy the sacred institutions and pervert the spiritual philosophies. Ulysses, who returns as a Hierophant of the Mysteries, destroys the suitors as Jesus scourged the money-lenders from the temple steps. Thus, after long struggling in the material state, Ulysses, the neophyte in metaphysical philosophy, accomplishes his find reunion with the sacred wisdom from which he went forth in his cycle of experiences. Homer invites students of the spiritual philosophies to follow this course, exclaiming:

"Haste, let us fly and all our sails expand, To gain our dear, our long-lost native land!"

Yours sincerely,

Manly P. Hall

SOME PHILOSOPHICAL FRAGMENTS
Supplement to Students Monthly Letter
HEALING - CHAPTER I

THE quest for health has again become an aspect of religion. Numerous cults have sprung up, which derive a great part of their income from the metaphysical treatment of disease. Grateful patients enrich these institutions for the real or imaginary help which they have received until today several such organizations flourish like the green bay tree. It seems no more than fair to the public in general and students of metaphysics in particular that the claims and pretensions of the various healing cults should be examined with an eye to the proper segregation of facts and fancies.

A ZOROASTRIAN PRAYER

"l praise the well-thought thoughts, well-spoken words, well-performed deeds. I lay hold on all good thoughts, good words, good deeds. I abandon all evil thoughts, evil words, evil deeds. I offer to you, Oh Ameshaspentas! praise and adoration, with good thoughts, good words, and good deeds, with heavenly mind, the vital strength of my own body."—From an ancient work.

In ancient times, all physicians were priests of the instituted Mysteries and, like the Asclepiads were attached to some shrine of the god of healing. When the material sciences divorced the occult arts, the physicians departed from the temples. They no longer sought divine assistance for the sick, but put their faith in poultices and physics. For nearly two thousand years, the medical profession purged and bled a suffering humanity and only within this present century has the healing art begun to sense its dependency upon spiritual and psychological factors.

Every physician of the ancient world was a priest and a philosopher. It was his duty to minister to the spiritual and mental needs as well as the physical necessities of his patient. Though a body be wracked with pain, the origin of that pain is not always in the body. The physician who is not a philosopher will lose many patients that a wise man might have saved. There are also diseases which only a spiritual counsellor can cure. The art of healing is more than materia medica. The art of healing has as its first and only consideration—the effecting of a cure. But unfortunately, materia medica places ahead of the patient's health a numerous array of medical prejudices and limits the practitioner to a few accredited but often ineffectual methods of treatment. In the last few years, the public has staged a successful revolution against pills. Natural methods of combating disease have been sponsored by a long-suffering human kind and the result has been a drastic change in the theory of therapeutics. Doctors, finding their medications unpopular, are more sparing of their prescriptions and drugs stores which not long ago catered exclusively to doctors opinions are dealing in books, hardware, cosmetics and chicken dinners. Even surgery has been affected by the general reformation. Whereas not long-ago operations were both numerous and lucrative, drugless healers and dieticians are now even successfully treating appendicitis, the old surgical standby, and saving no end of tonsils.

Under the influence of this rapid transformation in medical theory and practice, the doctors and surgeons are forming into two distinct classes. The first group is composed of the "stand-patters" and their solution to the problem is to exterminate all non "Medics" and in this way preserve the good old practice in the good old way—at the expense of the patient if necessary. The second group consisting of the forward-looking and progressive men are exploring the field of psychology and psychiatry, seeking the hidden causes of manifested things. These men, although somewhat school-bound, are taking an interest in the metaphysical aspects of heeding and are more or less honestly desirous of refounding the therapeutic theory upon something more substantial than a pillbox.

As far back as history records, there has been a supernatural element at work in the heeding arts. When physicians ceased to be priests, priests continued to be physicians. Nearly all old religious orders instructed their initiates in what we may call spiritual healing. The Pythagoreans healed by formulas, the Therapeuti, Nazarenes and Essenes by prayer, and several of the early Christian fathers by the "laying on of hands." As the church persecuted heretics for the sin of non-agreement, so the medical profession, since its inception has persecuted spiritual healers for the crime of non-conformity. In spite of this persecution, however, or possibly because of it, there has not been a single century since the Christian era in which well-authenticated cases of spiritual healing have not been recorded.

The nineteenth century brought with it a renaissance of ancient culture and belief. The spiritistic cults of the pagan world were reestablished under new names and the non-medical healing arts firmly refounded themselves in society. Before the century closed materia medica was not only aware of this competition but had felt keenly the inroads of such competition. In the twentieth century, the healing art may be said to consist of three important schools:

1st: the conservative and orthodox medical school.

2nd: the unorthodox and less conservative school the osteopaths, chiropractors, naturopaths, dieticians, psychiatrists, etc.

3rd: healers, "practitioners" organizations and individuals—usually without any scientific knowledge or background—practicing mental, spiritual or faith healing, magnetism, prayer, auto-suggestion and similar methods of inducing health.

Our present writing is devoted largely to the third group, for it is this group which, for the most part combines healing with religion. Entrenched behind the religious rights of the individual, various non-medical methods of treating disease are able to function which otherwise would fall easy prey to the legislations of the American medical board.

Metaphysical healing derives its authority directly from divine revelation. The founders of nearly all great religious movements, with the possible exception of Mohammed, are all accredited with possessing a supernatural power. In most cases miracles are attributed to them. What pious Christian would deny the power of faith over disease when their own Savior had raised the dead, opened the eyes of the blind, and had given to His disciple's power to heal the sick in His name? The problem of miracles leaves materia medica and theology in a deadlock. Although the Protestant clergy did not assert its privilege of treating disease by virtue of the admonition of its Founder, it was certainly sympathetic to the idea that God could bestow at His pleasure a curative virtue upon individuals untrained in medical science. Many of our medical specialists disagree, but must state their opinions in a modulated voice lest they lose patients.

We are now in an era of mystical movements. Dissatisfied with the literal interpretations of our spiritual canons, we are seeking to discover within the hard rind of dogma some richer meat. The desperate need for a more adequate spiritual code forces us into the mystical outlook and, with mysticism, inevitably comes healing. Mysticism is a mental Utopia. It is the Promised Land of theology. Mysticism is an escape from sordid literalism, and millions of people, disillusioned and disappointed, turn from the oppression of the outer world and seek release and solace in the building up of an inner mystical existence. It is natural that this trend should result in a critical attitude towards these materialistic institutions which are left behind. If it is a fact that the average material scientist has no patience with mystics, it is equally true that mystics have no patience with material scientists. If it be true that the materialistic scientists bigoted in his opinions, it is in equal measure true that the average student of metaphysics is bigoted in his mysticism. The doctor will say, "My hospital is full of individuals who ruin their lives through metaphysics!" And the metaphysical healer will say, "My sanatorium is filled with wreckage of medical ignorance!" There is some truth on both sides, and this makes the problem even more difficult to solve.

(To be continued)

PALINGENESIS OF PLANTS

PHOTOGRAPHIC REPRODUCTION OF ASTRAL PLANT LIFE ON FROSTED WINDOW PANES

A Reprint from "Star of the Magi" Dec. 1900.

A curious little pamphlet, bearing the explanatory title of "Frost Flowers on the Windows, the Result of Vital Energy of Plants," was issued some little time ago by a Chicago writer purposely to be circulated among the great scientific institutions and scientific journals of Europe and the United States. The author, Albert Alberg, who is well known in England and also somewhat in America as a writer for children, quite by chance, came upon a new light in psychic philosophy during the severe winter of 1899 in Chicago. He observed that the leaves of plants in particular photographed their structure on the frozen panes of windows. The first startling discovery was made at a restaurant, where he found that a number of puny celery stalks, left over from a dinner in their respective tumblers, had photographed themselves as ENTIRE celery plants, in their full growth and pulpy form in one long continuous row on four windows and also that some ferns had done likewise on a larger front window. This occurred on January 29, 1899.

Mr. Alberg perceived, at a glance, that the frost flowers were no mere freaks of "Jack Frost," as commonly accepted, but constituted a perfect system or process of Nature, where the psychic or soul life, so to speak, of the plant testified its existence in the delicate and often glorious display on the frosted windowpanes, a veritable palingenesis or resurrection of the plant in ice—an ice photography of the vital force of the plant, permeating the whole vegetable kingdom. He followed up this incipient indication and for several weeks made a number of startling discoveries and charming observations, enabling him, in a manner, to classify or systematize the whole floral frost display.

What Mr. Alberg noted may be briefly and concisely stated thus: If there be living plants in the rooms and there is a severe frost the plants will display their contours and even the ramifications of their fibers or network on the frosted windowpanes. If there are no living plants within, but such have recently been consumed therein, either by cooking or eating or smoking, you will invariably find just such leaves in the frost flowers. A cooked cabbage will produce a large cabbage leaf, cereals will give stunted grains with floss, frozen tobacco fumes will realize maimed tobacco leaves, and florists have their winter stock of greenery reproduced on their windows when the air inside is not too warm to admit of their icy reproduction. Yet still more startling discoveries were made—for instance, that woolen goods produce tall grass and foliage, such as the sheep have grazed upon, and that meat store windows and leather bindings displays will exhibit similar pasture herbage. But perhaps the most astonishing of all is that druggists' windows, and particularly saloon windows, where tropical ingredients in bottles occasionally uncorked, will surcharge the atmosphere to such an astounding degree that a rich tropical vegetable display is shown on the windows.

All these phenomena are on a somewhat magnified scale, with the exception of that of burning fir tree cordwood, when the redolent particles still lingering in the air in the room reproduce entire miniature fir trees in long rows, just as did the celery plants on the windows on an enlarged scale, with pulpy thickness. Among these observations noted are the following:

"The saloon, southeast corner of Sixtieth and State streets, was repapered on February 7. It being a very cold day the consequence was that at night the entire two large front windows were covered with an uncommonly thick layer of ice tracings of cereals, the effect of the paste used during the day. I drew the attention of the proprietor to it, who at once perceived the phenomenon of the powerful emanations of the cereals of which the paste was made. As I was curious I called again the following afternoon, when we both observed that nearly everywhere the tracings of cereals lay in uniform layers, just as the paperhanger's brush had affixed the paste on the long paper strips, by strokes right and left, which, however, had been effected in the adjoining back room, but having once been transfixed on the back of the paper, now in the big barroom, to judge by appearance, had evidently transmitted, by vibration, its influence on the large window glass panes, perhaps accelerated by the paperhanger's brush when smoothing down the paper on wall and ceiling. In the smokerooms ice tracings of tobacco leaves were plainly, visible during several cold days."

Another citation from Mr. Alberg's work presents a strong bit of evidence:

"Mrs. Charles Howard, a Theosophist of Chicago, after having heard a portion of this paper read, looked in her own house to see if she might discover any sign of ice palingenesis. She soon found an exemplar on a windowpane in front of which had chanced to be left a small jar of preserved grapes, in consequence of which a couple of large bunches of grapes had developed on the frosted window."

All these observations led Mr. Alberg to various philosophical speculations and deductions upon the psychic conditions of plants, and their relative connection with man. He says:

"From our observation of ice tracings, the frost seems in a manner to supply the means of an astral resurrection of plants, which Paracelsus and Dr. Hartmann refer to as being one of the secrets of the alchemists of bygone ages, for the plants plainly demonstrated by their ice palingenesis that they possess an innate power of extending their influence even into frost. With frost we generally associate death, just as with genial heat we associate life. But ice is not death, as witness the whole arctic regions, replete with cold-blooded animal life. Thus, then, we may infer that the frost flowers have been for the nonce imbued with life from their parent efflorescent plants, for else how would they have been called into existence? And exist they most certainly do. Do we not here stand face to face with another wonder of creation—ice palingenesis, or evolution of a plant into a frost flower counterpart, an ice shadow of its material ego, which could not have been called into existence had the parent plant no self-consciousness, no vital energy, no ego, no soul?"

"Thomas Edison holds that plants possess consciousness; some call it automatic consciousness. I am perfectly convinced of it. For instance, if you deprive a creeper of its support, it will soon send out an eager tendril to find another hold. Have the plants any object in thus repeating themselves in fancy ice tracings, or is it a mere freak of the plant, as we hitherto thought it was a freak of Frost? Depend upon it, there is no such thing as freak or chance in Nature, although the transient existence of the frost flowers may appear to us as purposeless as it is inexplicable to most of us. Yet they will occur again and again as often as opportunity affords, a bit of Nature, tiny and transient, I grant, but yet a phase of Nature, although hitherto ignored or laughed at. But from the attention drawn to the frost flowers I hope you will henceforth find them as interesting as heretofore you have found them, and always will find them exquisitely beautiful, and that you may try and find out their cause and their mission." Like the important discovery of the sexuality of plants by Linnaeus, Mr. Alberg's discovery has first been recognized in Sweden and Holland.

OCTOBER 1, 1934

From Metaphysics, which is the first grand department of philosophy, we must now pass on to Logic, the second major division.

Science has arisen not from the possession of fact but from the need of fact. Fact is finality. To possess it is to possess ultimate's of knowledge. As ultimate's of knowledge are impossible to man, fact is a term only. To gratify the natural egotism of the human creature, the term fact has been divided into the two terms, absolute fact and relative fact. Absolute fact is acknowledged but ignored, and upon the foundation of relative fact, the institutions of modern knowledge have been established.

Aristotle in some cases uses the term science as a synonym for knowledge, for he opposes science to ignorance. Science represents ordered knowledge or knowledge brought under the discipline of the reason. By knowledge is signified that which has been established by the testimony of the senses or demonstrated by the mind. Ignorance, as the antithesis of science, is the absence of knowledge.

There are three kinds of ignorance. The first Aristotle termed pure negation, or the condition of not knowing, which condition is natural to the child and the uninformed. The second form of ignorance Aristotle termed a depraved condition of the mind, as, for example, when the intellect is impoverished by false opinions or accepts untruths as knowledge. The third form of ignorance is compound ignorance. According to Plato and Confucius, a man who knows not and knows not that he knows not is afflicted with compound ignorance. This last form arises from untrained opinions fortified by egotism. Immaturity and lack of opportunity arc responsible for the natural forms of ignorance, but the more complex types of mental negation are due generally to perverse doctrines.

Logic is called the doctrine of reasonableness.

THE PRAYER OF CYRUS

"Thou Father Zeus, and Thou Sun, and all ye Gods, accept these sacrifices and thank offerings presented on account of the accomplishment of many and honorable works, and because you have pointed out to me both by sacrificial signs, and by signs in the heaven and by auguries, and by ominous messages, what things I ought, and what I ought not to do. Many thanks are also due to you, because I have also learned your watchful care, and have never in my season of prosperity been high minded above what becomes man. And now I beseech you to give happiness to my children, and wife, and friends, and country; and such a life as ye have granted me, so grant me a like death."—From an ancient work.

It was originally the science of reasoning itself, that is, it established the rules by which men should think. The history of logic is generally divided into two major periods: pre-Aristotelian and post Aristotelian. Aristotle was the founder of scientific logic and it is upon the premises laid down by him that the modern science of logic stands. To some measure, however, modern logic has been infected by the general tendency to complicate all systems and procedures. In its present state, logic is a confused mass of formulae and propositions of comparatively little value to the average layman.

Previous to the time of Aristotle, logic was termed "natural." Natural logic manifests as the tendency towards reasonableness which is inherent to all creatures possessing even the rudiments of intellect. Primitive peoples, the higher animals, and even under certain conditions plants, demonstrate the presence of logical impulse.

We disagree with the somewhat prevalent opinion that which is logical must, therefore, be true. That is logical which is consistent with its own premise, but if the premise be false, the conclusions which are reached may be logical to the premise and reasonable to the premise but lack fact because the premise was lacking in fact. The value of the logic, therefore, depends upon the integrity of the premises or elements. For example, we may take the premise: to be rich is virtuous, John is rich, therefore John is virtuous. The logic is all right, but the premise is wrong, and the chances are John is not virtuous.

It follows from this example that a certain knowledge of essential values is necessary to the logician. As essential values are metaphysical, it follows, logically, that metaphysics is necessary to logic. As the average modern logician is not a metaphysician and has no foundation in metaphysical values, logic becomes a war of words and a babel of formulae.

The tools or instruments of logic, according to Aristotle and the first masters of the science, are Analogy, Induction and Deduction. These philosophical instruments are of the greatest antiquity and are the original footings of the house of learning.

Analogy: is that form of inference which arises from the comparison of equals or of two particulars of similar import or magnitude. The Hermetic traditions of the Egyptians are exceedingly rich in examples of analogical inference.

Induction: is that form of inference which ascends from inferiors to superiors or which moves from particulars to universals; for example, from personality to principle.

Deduction: is that form of inference which descends from superiors to inferiors or from generals to particulars; for example, from infinites to finites.

It naturally follows that the human mind, when striving for a reasonable position, seeks to equilibrate itself by discovering its relationship with equals, superiors and inferiors. If it accomplishes this equilibrium through an intelligent use of the instruments of logic, that intellect may then be regarded as balanced.

We will now give examples of the three primary logical processes, using a simple formula, but all matters susceptible of logical examination may be subjected to the same treatment.

First, an example of analogy:

(a) It is wrong for John to steal;

(b) for Henry to steal is similar as for John to steal;

(c) therefore, it is wrong for Henry to steal.

This is called analogy because the two factors compared—John and Henry—are particulars of comparatively equal magnitude. This inference is susceptible of vast application. An evil which is practiced by one is equally evil to any other that is similar to that one, or in the same category.

Second, an example of induction:

(a) It is wrong for John to steal;

(b) all stealing is similar to John's stealing;

(c) therefore, all stealing is wrong.

In this case the inference ascends from particulars to generals. For John to steal is a particular; all stealing is a general or universal. By this process, an individual act is established as a measure of universal action. A particular that is evil establishes the evil of a universal of which that particular is an aspect or application.

Third, an example of deduction:

(a) All stealing is wrong;

(b) for John to steal is stealing;

(c) therefore, it is wrong for John to steal.

Here we have the example of descent from a universal to a particular. The principle of stealing is accepted as wrong, therefore, logically, all particular examples of theft being similar thereto, must be equally and particularly wrong.

Thus, by the three primary inferences, honesty is established as a logical conclusion. All scientific logic must be expressed in threefold formulas as above, but there are numerous ramifications of these formulae which lie beyond the province of our present treatment. It will be evident therefore that logic arises from comparisons and the creation of formulae which establish in reasonableness the matter under consideration.

The three processes of logic, just described, were greatly refined by Sir Francis Bacon, who is called the father of modern science, largely because of his emphasis upon the inductive processes of the mind. In this, Bacon perpetuated the canons of Aristotle as opposed to the deductive methods of Pythagoras and Plato.

Metaphysically speaking, we may assume that philosophy, per se, arises out of the analogical inferences of logic; science arises out of the inductive processes of logic; and religion out of the deductive processes of logic. Theology reasons downward from generals to particulars, making the will of God the law of man and viewing all of the particulars of life as dominated by universal principles. Science, on the other hand, establishes its foundation upon known things and seeks to discover God from inferences based upon particulars; therefore, all that science suspects concerning the vastness of the universe extending beyond the physical perceptions is based upon conclusions derived from an analysis of seen and tangible objects. Philosophy occupies a sort of middle distance. It is the rational equalizer. Philosophy recognizes neither superiors nor inferiors in the last analysis but regards all appearances of superiority and inferiority as merely manifestations or aspects of equitable principles.

The science of logic has certain utilitarian aspects. This is more apparently true in the older schools of thought. We live in an age of speculative sciences. The operative arts of the ancients find a small place in modern philosophies. Intelligent living is the application of the various energies of man to their legitimate ends. Speculative science discovers, operative science applies.

The logical processes are the foundations of mental consistency and certain forms of consistency are necessary to rational thought in spite of Emerson's often quoted opinion on the subject. Inasmuch as logic is so closely related to what we term consistency, it may be well to define the word consistency in the terms of classical philosophy.

All thought must have continuity. It must move sequentially along lines of reasonable inference. A rational mental viewpoint does not arise merely from an accumulation of opinions or ideas. The mental life must be planned; thoughts must be built up according to a plan and a law; there must be direction and purpose. Consistency infers reasonable relationships between ideas and actions. It infers an orderly sequence in the process of applying thought to action. Emerson condemned consistency because he felt that it limited and narrowed the viewpoint, imposing certain scholastic limitations upon man's freedom to think. Emerson believed that every man should preserve the right to change his mind. He saw no virtue in binding the mind of the unborn tomorrow with the opinions of the dead yesterday. In this, he was perfectly correct. We too often feel it is a sacred and patriotic duty to perpetuate worn-out and out-grown beliefs. Progress arises usually from courage of conviction. Very often we must dare to be different in the face of established precedent. For some reason, not altogether clear, the word consistency has come to be associated with mental conservativeness when in reality the word actually infers no such intellectual limitation.

A person may change his mind every day and still be perfectly consistent. He may cling to old dogmas throughout a lifetime and still be utterly inconsistent. A man who outgrows an old belief and grasps a broader concept should not be branded inconsistent because he has changed his mind. He is inconsistent only if he tries to reconcile the new and the old and live a compromise between them. Growth is a process which creates a constant need for adjustment in life and viewpoint. Growth demands an improvement in the entire nature and not merely an extension of power in someone part of the nature. Inconsistency arises when part of the mind believes one thing and another part of the mind believes another thing, and the two beliefs are perpetuated together, resulting in irreconcilable contradictions of thought. When your mind changes, your whole life must change with it. If you believe in new things, you must live in a new way in harmony with those beliefs. Thus, consistency may be defined as agreement or concord, a logical relationship.

Logic is the term peculiarly applicable to the continuity of ideas. By use of its principles, the intellect moves logically from a premise to its logical inferences; these inferences, in turn become conclusions, and these conclusions become new premises. This process continues along logical and, if the logic is correct, reasonable lines. The term consistent should not be applied to this process, but rather to the results arising from this process. The term consistent is applicable only to the consequences of logic. For example, through a chain of logic, the mind establishes the reasonableness of honesty. We could never say that honesty is consistent or inconsistent, or that the processes by which it is established in the mind are consistent or inconsistent. Honesty is a virtue established by logic, justified by experience and observation, and its desirability is acceptable to the reason. Honesty, however, is an abstract term which must be interpreted by each individual according to his or her personal standard of integrity. Thus, honesty gives rise in action to certain particular codes of personal action. Throughout civilization, the standards of virtue and honesty have been subjected to constant change. In Sparta, for example, thievery was a virtue. As we grow and evolve our standards of right and wrong gradually unfold, but all normal persons have a standard of honesty demonstrable by logic. To the degree that we violate our own standards, to that degree, we are inconsistent in action. We are not inconsistent because we change our attitude; we are inconsistent because we fail to live up to our standard whatever it may be.

Premises may be logical or illogical but never consistent or inconsistent. Action, based upon these premises, can be consistent or inconsistent, but never logical or illogical.

To briefly summarize the uses of logic: By logical means, we can order the mental processes we live by. We can establish a justifiable code upon which to find character, and which will serve to secure the life of the individual. Energy wasted in useless friction can never be put to any good end. We cannot face life with courage and certainty while we live codes, we have never proved to ourselves and justified by a proper intellectual criterion. Having arrived at logical conclusions concerning those spiritual values which are the foundation of our well-being, let us live consistently with these conclusions, bringing our life into a coordinated and harmonious pattern. Think well and live in harmony with your thoughts. Think logically and live consistently.

Yours sincerely,
Manly P. Hall

944 West 20th Street.
Los Angeles, Calif.

HEALING - CHAPTER II

IN the old mythological theologies, diseases were said to have been visited upon mankind by the gods in punishment for the disobedience to divine edicts. If we interpret these fables in the Orphic manner, we must view "the gods" as the various aspects of natural law, through disobedience to which humanity brings down upon itself reactions of sickness and death. Thus, to the philosophers man himself, through the unwisdom of his thoughts and actions, is the direct cause of all the evils which afflict him. Knowledge of the divine plan and obedience to the divine edicts are the foundations of health and the only panacea for the world's woe. Immoderation due to ignorance then is the true cause of most mortal ills.

Immoderation is unbalance and without true spiritual understanding the human creature is incapable of preserving that equilibrium in all his parts which is essential to good health. The wise ones of old who enjoyed the "philosophic extension of years" achieved their comparative immunity from physical ills through a moderation of all the extremes of thought and action, living according to what Aristotle calls the Golden Mean, that is "in all things not too much." This is called temperance. As all the progress in civilization is accomplished in the temperate zones of the earth so all individual progress must be accomplished in the temperate zones of living. But only the wise are temperate and the wise are few.

As health was originally corrupted through intemperance, so, though it be restored, it will be corrupted again until the cause of the corruption be removed. True health is accordingly possible only to those who live according to the laws of life. For the rest of mankind there must be constant alternations between growth and decay, between health and disease. No man can actually BE well until he thinks well, lives well and acts well. Thus, philosophy is the highest form of medicine, and the philosopher is the greatest of all physicians.

This is the true theory of health upon which all metaphysical systems of healing must be established. To the degree that they depart from this premise or are inconsistent with it to that degree they depart from and are inconsistent with reason and common sense. The physician must be more than a doctor of ills; he must be a builder of character; he must direct the resources of his patient to a more perfect method of living and thinking.

According to the priest, physicians of antiquity the intemperance's arising from ignorance and causing disease manifest through seven categories of ailments. Each of these categories must be studied by the physician and his treatment adapted to the peculiarities of each. These categories are as follows.

1st: PHYSICAL DISEASE. Under this heading are grouped all such maladies as corrupt the flesh, inhibit function, destroy structure and finally bring about disintegration of the corporeal body. To the doctor of meteria medica nearly all diseases are regarded as physical but to the philosopher physician diseases are but a small part of sickness. Physical disease must be divided into two general classes.

(a) Such as have their origin directly in the body itself.

(b) Such as are communicated to the body either from the environment without or the super physical parts of man within.

The physical body, being merely an instrument of the emotions and the mind, can seldom be regarded as an actual cause of disease but rather is the victim of mental, emotional and physical intemperance's. By physical intemperance, we mean those which originate from the physical impulses of the mind. Once a mental or emotional intemperance has caused a malady in the flesh, it becomes necessary to regard a disease in a twofold aspect and it is often necessary to treat both the cause and the effect. Physical disease may arise from the breaking of a spiritual, mental, or physical law and should be treated accordingly.

When it is evident that a physical law is the one which has been transgressed, either through ignorance or accident, such as lack of hygiene in the first case or some poisoning in the second, physical treatments are indicated. It is worse than folly to treat uncleanliness with affirmations or poisonings with platitudes. In fact, it verges on the sacrilegious to enlist divine aid where only human common sense is necessary. It is also folly to take medicines when they are not needed or to refuse them when necessary. Those who disapprove of medicines should know that even food itself is medicine for hunger. A man may boast that he will never enter a chemist's shop, but he has a chemist's shop within himself wherein the chemical elements of food are prepared that they may be easily assimilated into the tissues of the bodily fabric. While it is unquestionably true that many medicines are more dangerous than the disease they are intended to cure, it is also true that the wisest of the initiated physicians made use of herbs and poultices, and a good physic has saved many a life. It is always desirable to protect the body from the corrosive effect of powerful and dangerous drugs; but in this progressive century there are ample methods of working with physical disease which are both effective and when properly administered safe. Osteopathy, chiropractic, naturopathy, dietetics, physiotherapy, hydrotherapy, Spectro chrome therapy and numerous other similar therapeutic methods have been successfully developed and applied. These, combined with common sense, and medicine where absolutely necessary, will prolong life and efficiency.

A word about surgery. In rare cases, surgery is the only method by which life can be preserved. Under such conditions, surgery is certainly justified. Willful failure to use every reasonable means to preserve health and life is equal to suicide.

Under the heading of physical disease must be included, such ills as are not pathological nor functional but arise from accidents and injuries. These require immediate treatment and only a fanatic will refuse his body those aids necessary to its survival.

2nd: EMOTIONAL DISEASES. Under this heading must be classified such ailments as having their origin in emotional intemperance, but which may later infect the physical fabric. Emotion generally destroys order, procedure, sequence, and coordination of parts. It renders the life dependent upon feeling. The individual responds immoderately to impulses of pleasure and displeasure. Real values are lost sight of and the life is dedicated to the service of imminent impulse. Such persons possess strong sympathies but are weak in the control of them. We all know "gushy" and sentimental persons whose hearts are in the right place but who are utterly lacking in discrimination, poise and foresight.

Sentimentalism can become a disease and, contributing its erratic quality to the body, generally produces acute nervous conditions and numerous psycho-physical complexes detrimental to the biological economy. When such a person seeks health, it is the physician's duty to emphasize the absolute necessity for poise and emotional discipline. These people must build reasonable foundations under their feelings so that they live by directed thought and not by undirected reflex. Various physical treatments may temporarily restore a semblance of bodily harmony, but the stress of immoderate sentimentalism will leave its scars in the tissues and will tear down the bodily health as quickly as it is restored. Many religious institutions foster emotionalism, whipping the sentiments by a carefully planned theological theatricalism.

Persons inclined to uncontrollable emotionalism should never frequent places where there is emotional display. These people should also work industriously to attain detachment, for nearly all emotional people are desperately attached to persons or ideas.

This attachment adds to the nervous strain and prevents relaxation. Emotional people should also be constantly watchful of inhibitions for suppressed emotionalism often leads to desperate consequences. In attempting to correct emotional unbalance, never deny the existence of the sentiments or attempt to control them by a strong action of the will. Rather seek, to outgrow them by building in a sufficient structure of intellectual perspective so that the excess of feeling will cease of its own accord, being neutralized by intelligent thinking. The physician wording with such cases must have long patience with which to listen and good advice with which to assist the patient out of his emotional complexes.

3rd: THE PASSIONAL DISEASES. The passions of man differ from his emotions because of the violence with which they are directed to the accomplishment of some definite purpose. Emotions are more or less scattered and static, but passions are usually coordinated and dynamic.

Of the passions, probably the most powerful is ambition, which is one of the chief destroyers of human life. Ambition, which is a constant drive to a position of power, is an immoderate passion to which is usually sacrificed all of the worthwhile things of life. Nearly all of the world's so-called great men are sick, for the constant striving after material gain exhausts the energies and impoverishes the soul. The physician should attempt to direct the mind of the patient towards the improvement of his inner life and to the realization that it is nobler to become wise than it is to possess things or express power.

Another powerful passional disease manifests through sexual intemperance or abnormality. This field is too great to be covered in so short a writing and where it is presumed to exist it should be immediately studied by a qualified psycho-analyst. The sexual energy lies at the root of all human progress and it should not be destroyed but should be lifted as far as possible from the level of animal instinct to the plane of creative endeavor. Under all circumstances the physician must work towards normalcy and moderation, realizing that all complexes rise from misuse.

A third and very prevalent passional disease is appetite. Inordinate appetites gratified at the expense of the bodily harmony must always result in deterioration of the physical fabric. Moderation of living is simplicity and, all things being equal, he is happiest who limits his appetites to that which is necessary. Again, spiritual healing is of very little use in correcting the evils brought about by physical indulgence. The problem is simply one in self-control. No man has a right to expect to enjoy good health who cannot, to a reasonable degree, subdue his appetites and continue in a state of temperance. The greatest boon which nature can bestow is health, and she reserves this reward for those who live reasonably and rationally.

Under the heading of passional disease are also to be included anger, hate, greed, lust, jealously and all such violent and destructive emotions as wrack the soul and corrode the flesh. No person can expect his body to be free from poisons if his mind is filled with them. We sometimes think that we do another a great harm by hating him when in reality he is indifferent to our dislike and we canker only ourselves. No one has a right to be either healthy or happy in whose soul resides destructive animosities. Cleanse first the soul of its passions and, in most cases, there will be observed a rapid improvement in the physical health. We make ourselves ill by our own misdeeds and it is only fair and right that we should make ourselves well again by the correction of these evils. No man who has not purified his own life should seek health from his physician.

4th: MENTAL DISEASES. What we are is in great measure the result of what we think- When we speak of mental disease, we do not necessarily infer what is commonly meant by insanity. Rather, we mean destructive systems of thinking which turn the life awry. The mind was given to man that by it he might direct his actions and guard from excess the lesser parts of himself. The whole life which we live here is dominated by our mental attitudes. If these attitudes be unworthy or destructive, the entire existence is clouded, and we live by a code inferior to that proper for man. The mind is a precious instrument by the right use of which we distil experience from action, build character and elevate ourselves to an almost divine estate. It is the mind alone of all the faculties, of man which is capable of discovering moderation. An old philosopher once said: "An enlightened mind in a human body is the greatest in the least."

The purpose of education is to ensure the health of the mind, but as most modern educational systems are devoted solely to materialistic culture, the mind from childhood is denied several forms of knowledge essential to its well-being. When the mind is trained to a point of true discrimination, the thinker becomes a sage. Mind, like all other parts of the material man, has, however, boundaries and limitations and wisdom dictates that these be properly understood. A man who makes less than proper use of his mind is less than a man; a man who makes more than proper use of his mind endangers the integrity of his thinking equipment. For example, lack of sufficient mental exercise leaves the mind slow and unresponsive and usually brutal and inconsistent, but if the mind on the other hand is over-exerted and focused upon problems beyond its capacity, its faculties are impaired, thoughts are confused and mania may follow. Between these two extremes is that divine moderation by which the intellect, preserved from corruption and directed towards truth, through its gradual unfoldment elevates the whole personality to a philosophic life.

Those excesses which disease the mind arise out of ignorance and perversion. Disease due to ignorance include various opinionisms which Heraclitus so well defined: "A falling sickness of the intellect." Also under this heading are various fallacies of the educational system by which the mind is wrongly trained in values. Also, unsound philosophies and theologies by which the thinking may be unduly influenced and reason obscured by prejudice and misdirected zeal. Of that class of mental disease due to perversion are such as those by which thought power is willfully directed to an unworthy end as schemes, plots, intrigues, and all systems of mental exploitation, in which thought becomes an instrument of unfair advantage. Our whole industrial civilization is rife with examples of mis-directed mind force. A man who secretly plots against the common good or raises empire upon deceits and fanaticism for profit must not be surprised if his physical health is destroyed by his evil practices. For such a man to ask divine assistance for his physical ills is worse than sacrilege, for it is written in the law that no man may sow evil and reap good.

5th: DISEASES DUE TO IMAGINATION. What Plato calls the imaginative aspect of the human soul is the abode of phantoms and chimera. Imagination arises out of the chemical relationship between the known and the unknown. The small intellectual sphere of man is immersed in a limitless expanse of the unknown. Where reason leaves off imagination begins. Imaginations arise from the unassimilated elements of religion, tradition, and experience. Morbid imaginations are nightmares of our waking hours, usually founded upon some small part of truth, greatly distorted and out of perspective. A morbid imagination can destroy the whole complexion of life and where it exists may generally be accepted as the cause of such physical ills as are present. Examples of morbid imagination may range anywhere from distrust of people to melancholia and fears of insanity.

One of the least suspected forms of imagination is that which assigns miraculous origins and purposes to perfectly ordinary and prosaic circumstances. The physicist seeks for a natural, physical origin to everything; the metaphysician seeks for a supernatural, metaphysical origin for everything. It is unreasonable to maintain that the material universe was founded without reason, perpetuated without intellect and destroyed without hope, but it is also unreasonable to attribute a toothache to the devil, black magic, secret enemies or the personal animosity of God. Each of these conclusions in its own field is an example of morbid imagination. When the mind begins looking for the supernatural, it has little difficulty in discovering miracles. If this same mind lacks a sound foundation in the philosophy of metaphysics, it soon involves itself in a hopeless muddle of demons, sprites, goblins and sorceries. All these things are the stuff that manias are made from.

(To be continued)

NOVEMBER 1, 1934

Dear Friend,

In last month's letter we attempted to show how philosophy, as logic, established the reasonableness or unreasonableness of mental premises through a definite procedure. This month we shall attempt to show how philosophy, as ETHICS, examines the moral value of thought and action.

Ethics is generally defined as the science of morality; but this definition, like so many others in the field of abstract learning, must not be taken too literally. In practice, ethics is the science of attempting to understand morality. The whole subject of morality is susceptible of division into two major aspects. The first of these parts seeks to answer the question: what is morality? The second seeks the answer to the question: what ought morality to be?

The question: what is morality? It is generally answered by a survey of the moral codes and statutes of various civilizations, past and present. This survey reveals the social outworking of the moral impulse in man. As we have no way of examining the moral impulse, except by a consideration of its consequences, we judge morality by morals, even as we judge the quality of minds by the thoughts which emanate from them. A rather comprehensive review of morality is therefore not difficult to secure, as long as we are satisfied to estimate causes entirely by their effects.

The question of what morality ought to be is, unfortunately, far more abstract and difficult to answer. We all know what we do, but we are not all so certain of what we should do. Morality is a code of relationships. It is that part of philosophy which estimates the importance of one person's actions upon another person. There has always been a wide interval between theory and practice in human relationships. Although civilization is generally regarded as a moral empire, its codes have not produced individual or collective security. Therefore, the true ends of morality have not been achieved. An example of the abstract issue of morality is patriotism. Most nations regard patriotism as a moral virtue, yet patriotism, as now interpreted, is often anti-social and destructive. Thus, we see that the question of what is patriotism, if examined in the light of accepted tradition, might be answered with the words "fanatical nationalism." If, on the other hand, we ask the question: what ought patriotism to be? We should have to answer it in some more noble strain, possibly with the definition "love of man." In the words of Thomas Paine, "The world is my country."

Of course, it is necessary, in approaching the problem of ethics, to establish some standard of action. This standard becomes the accepted measure of morality. Unfortunately, there are fundamental differences of opinion as to what constitutes moral standards. These opinions may be classified under four general headings.

1st: Theologians maintain that the will of God is the standard of morality; that the Scriptural books of the world, because they are accepted as containing the revealed Word of God, are the absolute textbooks of morality.

2nd: The rationalists maintain that pure reason is the ultimate criterion of morality; that philosophy, by extending all moral values to their abstract ultimate's of perfection, reveals the code of action that all men should strive for.

3rd: The hedonists take the ground that comfort, pleasure and utility should be the dominating factors in morality; that, individually and collectively, we should perform those actions which are most pleasant and least arduous and cause the least social confusion. Many of the adherents to this system view the more conservative codes of moralism as merely religious inhibitions.

4th: The biologists assume that morality is a perfect adjustment to natural law and social environment. To this school, naturalness is the chief of the virtues; and a person who lives a standard perfectly consistent with what he is, in terms of species and type, may be regarded as a moral animal. The biologists, however, do assume that natural law to some measure involves community responsibility. The biological definition of morality is, therefore, perfect biological adaptation to environment and circumstance.

In addition to these four rather well-defined interpretations of ethics, there is a fifth abstract approach to the subject. By this approach, morality is made a synonym of perfection. Perfectionism is defined as the ethics of self-realization. This interpretation defines morality as a purely personal issue. Right and wrong are regarded as individual problems, and morality consists of each individual living his own code according to his own light; at the same time presuming the existence of a natural impulse in man, which is leading him to a rational and constructive philosophy of life.

One of the great problems peculiarly within the province of ethics is the origin of the so-called moral urge. Is there something within man impelling him to the right action, or is morality merely the outgrowth of primitive social relationship? In other words, is there an absolute standard of right and wrong in the universe, or is there merely a relative standard arising from action? Again, does the moral urge derive its authority from what is commonly termed universal law? Is this universal law the conscious Will of the Creative Agent, or is it merely the mechanistic procedure of a universal agency? Is there a universal consciousness of morality, or is morality only an accident of human consciousness arising out of human chemistry?

The intuitionalists assume that the human mind becomes aware, through a mystical extension of consciousness, of a vast universal morality by which man should regulate his life. The materialists, on the other hand, contend that there is no moral certainty in existence and that all action is finally motivated by impulses toward survival. Another definition of morality, therefore, is the code of survival. Experience, over vast periods of time, has justified certain attitudes towards action and demonstrated the necessity of certain relationships. These actions and relationships constitute the so-called moral evidences in life. Ethics is the science of these actions and relationships, and the purpose of philosophy is to understand and apply them.

All human beings naturally desire to be happy and all justifiable moral codes must, in some measure, acknowledge the desirability of this end. Ethics divides happiness into two forms. The first it terms egotistic, and the second universalistic. Egotistic happiness, as a code of ethics, seeks the comfort, security and pleasure of the individual, and under its law each man places his own well-being as the first consideration of life. Universalistic happiness, as a code of ethics, identifies the happiness of the individual with collective happiness.

Nearly all of the great philosophers, mystics and prophets, of the world have been dominated by the universalistic theory of happiness. To the wise man, the happiness of each depends upon the happiness of all. From a moral standpoint, unselfishness is regarded as a more refined emotion than selfishness; therefore, universalistic ethics is regarded as superior and more enlightened than egotistic ethics. The materialist, however, will immediately ask: by what rule do we posit unselfishness as superior to selfishness? This immediately plunges the mind into the deepest parts of the moral issue. If we accept ethics as a philosophy of conduct, we must then define right conduct. According to philosophical morality, right conduct is that system of action that most completely meets human need and leads towards the realization of the most noble human aspiration. It would follow, as Immanuel Kant has observed, that ethics leads to that ultimate condition in which individuals live together in a condition of ends, rather than in a state of means. All action is a means towards an end. When the right action accomplishes the end, then we pass from the state of effort to the state of reward. Happiness is defined as that condition of consciousness which man enjoys when he has fulfilled the requisite actions to produce happiness. The old masters of ethical philosophy postulated the Golden Age as that time which was to come, when all morality as means had accomplished morality as ends; and men dwelt together in a social order arising out of moral discipline and the permanent establishment of moral values.

To students of metaphysical philosophy, the issues of ethics must be developed along lines of metaphysical inference. At the same time, the physical inferences cannot be ignored; they should be regarded as Plato regarded them, as suspended from spiritual causes. The initiated Pagans regarded ethics as one of the seven major attributes of divinity. God was not only spirit and body, but also soul, and the term soul inferred the whole sphere of moral virtues. Socrates declared God to be good, thus positing morality as an inevitable correlative of divinity.

The word "good" is a very abstract term and is impossible of exact definition. It is almost certain to be involved in opinion when defined. Therefore, like truth, it is divided into an absolute and a relative aspect. The absolute aspect is ignored as impossible of understanding, and its relative aspect is defined in terms of existing standards, inferring honesty, virtue, obligation, etc. We live in an age of exploitation, in which might exercise its temporal advantage over right, and the issues of morality are confused by the despotism of advantage. The will of the strong becomes the passing standard of right and wrong. Conquerors make laws for the conquered, and the uninformed ascribe to these laws a universal aspect which they do not merit. In time, errors long perpetuated become custom. Men no longer examine them, but accept unquestioning old edicts and ancient fallacies.

It is inconceivable, as Francis Bacon has observed, that this great universal plan should be without a soul. We are constantly confronted with irrefutable evidence of a directing Intellect. If there is consciousness in man, there is consciousness in the universe of which man is but so small a part. If there is morality in man, there is but one source from which he can have derived it, and that is from the Sovereign Morality of the world.

Plato was unquestionably one of the noblest men who has ever lived upon this earth. The theology of Plato is one of the most exalted religious systems ever established in the world. There is no better way to approach the philosophy of Ethics than through a series of definitions Platonically set forth. You will remember from our previous letter that the logic of Plato descended from generals to particulars, from universal concepts to specific applications. The Platonic philosophy is developed from these fundamental premises.

1: That Universal Cause, which men have named God, is Divine Life, to which the qualities of consciousness, intelligence and virtue are intrinsic.

2: God is good; that is, Divinity, by virtue of its own existence and its own nature, is by necessity the standard of absolute perfection, to which all other things must conform if they are to be god-like.

3: It therefore follows that, all who participate of God as Energy or Mind must also participate of God as Virtue, as these qualities are indivisible and essentially one.

4: In the process of growth, or evolution, forms partake of Divinity first as energy or consciousness; second as intelligence or mind; and third as virtue or morality. It follows that virtue is one of the last of human achievements, for creatures possessing life and intelligence do not necessarily possess virtue. Virtue, while latent in all natures, is said to be possessed when it is objectified in action. Thus, we may say that a being possesses, or does not possess, virtue in the sense that it either manifests, or does not manifest, virtue in individual action.

5: Life energizes, intellect organizes, virtue civilizes. Thus, all of the constructive relationships, by which isolated creatures are finally brought into a cooperative community existence, arise from man's realization of Divinity as virtue.

6: Virtue is demonstrated on several planes of nature, but it must never be confused with various human emotions. Love, friendship, mercy, obligation, responsibility, generosity, etc. are terms often confused with virtue. It should be remembered that virtue is a principle. We may call it, for practical purposes, the principle of right relationships. Any constructive emotion may or may not be virtuous according to its intrinsic merit, for virtue is a principle and not an action. Generosity, for example, is not a virtue in itself, but it becomes a virtue when directed by wisdom and integrity. Impractical generosity can in no way be regarded as a virtue.

7: Thus, it appears that action partakes of virtue, to the degree that it is consistent with that universal fitness which is the very foundation of the world.

8: Platonically considered, virtue is more than morality, for morality is limited to creatures possessing a moral nature, whereas virtue exists as a principle beyond the sphere of moral values. Ethics, consequently, goes beyond morality and includes that aspect of the Divine purpose, which is suggested by the term "fitness."

9: We must now define fitness. As we examine the universal plan, as it is manifest in the universe spread out before us, we must be particularly impressed by the rightness and orderliness everywhere manifest. To use a homely simile, there seems to be a place for everything and everything is in its place. The parts work together; the diversity is enclosed within an all-sufficient unity; cooperation is everywhere present. Contemplating the mystery of Divine order, we cannot fail to be impressed with a certain sense of substantial fitness. Everything is where it ought to be, doing what it ought to do. This must be the pattern of all human relationships. Thus, ethics is man where he ought to be, doing what he ought to do, synchronizing personal purpose with universal purpose.

10: Immanuel Kant gives a lofty definition of ethics in his famous categorical imperative. He realized that each man must so act that, if that man's action became a universal law, it would be just and sufficient. The true student of ethics bows to the inevitable spiritual realities of life. He realizes that obedience to universal law is the beginning of individual fitness.

Morality is generally involved in the problem of good and evil, and numerous man-made codes of right and wrong are confused with ethics. All right and wrong must be measured by the law of universal fitness and not by man-made codes. When an individual, through ignorance, violates some principle of universal fitness, he suffers. When a community violates the universal principle of community relationships, that community falls into evil, even though its man-made laws are not transgressed. Man is happy and his world is at peace when he lives in harmony with universal purpose. It is a universal purpose which reveals natural ethics. To the philosopher, fitness not only infers rightness but the "fitting in" quality. We are virtuous when we "fit in" to, the law of life. We are moral when we live in perfect attunement with the plan of which we are a part. This plan is not only a physical plan, but a mental and spiritual plan. When our spiritual life is consistent with the spiritual purpose of being, when our mental life is in harmony with the laws of mind, and when our physical life is consistent with the laws of nature, we may then regard ourselves as ethical creatures, possessing virtue and morality.

Yours sincerely,

Manly P. Hall

944 West 20th Street.
Los Angeles, Calif.

HEALING - CHAPTER III

(Continued from Oct. better Supplement)

Occult philosophy is not suited for small capacities and when little minds grasp at great subjects, there is usually much misunderstanding to say the least. To imagine oneself the victim of an endless chain of infernal necromancies or to feel oneself the incarnation of a demigod must lead to disastrous complexes. If students of metaphysics could realize that the whole universe is ruled by law and order and that a sovereign good directs it all, they would know without question that while small ills may temporarily obscure the divine purpose, in time and eternity all things work together for good. It is the duty of man to conquer the unknown through intelligent effort and not to sit shivering in the darkness of ignorance, bestowing a malevolent intent upon every shadow.

Whatever we believe, no matter how ridiculous, we can quickly find evidence to support. We read into books what we want to find there and we perceive in life that which we desire to perceive. Thus, an imagination complex, once established, gathers momentum with every passing year until it seems to the unfortunate person who has it that the whole universe testifies to his superstition.

There is a fine line of demarcation between imagination and clairvoyance and many persons who believe that they have actually experienced spiritual phenomena have really only suffered from a highly aggravated attack of imagination. It has been our observation that most people who say they have metaphysical experiences have experiences similar to those which they have recently read in books or have overheard at some gossip mart.

THE PRAYER OF FIRMICUS

"But lest my words be bereft of divine aid and the envy of some hateful man impugn them by hostile attacks, whoever thou art, God, who continuest day after day the course of the heavens in rapid rotation, who perpetuatest the mobile agitation of oceans tides, who strengthenest earth's solidity in the immovable strength of its foundation, who refreshest with night's sleep the toil of our earthly bodies, who when our strength is renewed returnest the grace of sweetest light, who stirrest all the substance of thy work by the salutary breath of the winds, who pourest forth the waves of streams and fountains in tireless force, who revolvest the varied seasons by sure periods of days: sole Governor and Prince of all, sole Emperor and Lord, whom all the celestial forces serve, whose will is the substance of perfect work, by whose faultless laws all nature is forever adorned and regulated; thou Father alike and Mother of everything, thou bound to thyself, Father and Son, by one bond of relationship; to Thee we extend suppliant hands, Thee with trembling supplication we venerate; grant us grace to attempt the explanation of the courses of thy stars; thine is the power that somehow impels us to that interpretation. With a mind pure and separated from all earthly thoughts and purged from every stain of sin, we have written these books for thy Romans."

They are perfectly sincere, perhaps, in believing that they have actually passed through a mystical experience but an overwrought imagination resulted in the deceit. Generally speaking, true clairvoyants are not emotional people, nor are they uninformed dabblers in the shallows of metaphysics. When we find a strongly emotional and almost hysterical person who is constantly "seeing things" or is perfectly certain that he or she is a focal point for supernatural circumstances, we must conclude that it is either a problem in imagination or in negative mediumship. Most probably it will be the former.

The diseases arising from imagination are usually morbid hallucinations often verging into hysteria and sometimes leading into forms of insanity. The physical results are often reflected into the glandular chain, affect the sympathetic nervous system and bring about devitalization and anemia. These conditions, in turn open the body to infections and contagions and reduce the recuperative power.

6th: DISEASES DUE TO HABIT. The mind with the least number of habits is capable of the greatest amount of constructive thinking. Habits prejudice the intellect causing a form of dishonesty which is certain to influence all decisions. Habits come under two general classifications; the first we may call racial or environmental, and the second individual or innate. A very good example of an unfortunate racial habit in religion is the King James version of the Holy Bible. This translation teems with errors and is hopelessly unreliable from a scholastic viewpoint, yet popular acceptance has caused this mis-version of holy writ to come to be recognized as infallible so that the religious public would now reject a correct translation. In fact, it has already shown its attitude in the matter by refusing a revised edition. For over 300 years, erroneous theological notions have been circulated, deriving their authority from the King James translation of the Bible. Christendom has been the loser and prejudice triumphs over truth. Habits and precedents are constantly persecuting originality and progress. Most people coming into metaphysical lines of thinking bring with them at least a subconscious strata of ecclesiastical prejudice. New thought may be in their heads, but orthodoxy is in their bones. They accept new ideas and often sincerely seek to apply them but in nearly every case the old opinions crop out, until modern metaphysics in its present form is a sort of compromise between classical paganism and mid-Victorian orthodoxy. Modern orthodox Christendom and the ancient philosophical religions are utterly irreconcilable, and he who tries to mingle them together in a broad-minded eclecticism creates a mass of contradictions within himself. An effort to live this compromise is dangerous if not fatal. No one can live more than one system of philosophical thinking at a time. We may appreciate all of them and study them, but we cannot apply their disciplines indiscriminately. A great number of metaphysical students consider it broad-minded to be Cabbalistic on Monday, Vedantic on Tuesday, Platonic on Wednesday, Yogis on Thursday, Mohammedan on Friday, Christian on Saturday and Zoroastrians on Sunday. At the same time, they are also dominated by a subjective orthodoxy to someone of the numerous Christian cults or isms. It might not seem that such a procedure would have a destructive effect on the health, but it has been definitely demonstrated that it has. A system of religious belief has a distinct vibration of its own and acceptance of that belief produces a definite chemical change in the structure of the body. The combining of these various chemistries without law or plan destroys the bodily equilibrium, unseats the intellect, and works a strain upon the whole psycho-nervous structure. We may be tolerant of all beliefs, inform ourselves in their philosophies and principles, but the purpose of such instruction is thwarted if we allow the various teachings to remain in the mind as a muddle of undigested material. We should never study more than we can classify and use. If we do, we shall suffer from mental indigestion, which, incidentally, is a very real and serious disease.

The pathology of habit has many aspects. Civilization is a habit, our methods of thinking are habits, our clothes are habits, the way we eat is a habit, our laws are habits and our attitudes towards success and failure are among the most pernicious of our habits. Nearly all these habits arise from precedent and custom and though they be uncomfortable and even detrimental to us we accept them as inevitable elements in our life. It is quite certain that such an array of habits will infect our philosophies. This is definitely evident in the modern realistic schools springing up in France and Germany. When habits affect our philosophies, they affect our lives; when habits affect our lives they affect our health, and when they affect our health, the consideration and classification of them must be a part of the healing art. So, when a man is sick, we should study his habits, not only mental but physical, not only individual but those of the social strata from which he comes. We shall discover in civilization itself idiosyncrasies and inconsistencies which become chemical factors in the health of races.

To return for a moment to the problem of affirmation and denial as taught by certain metaphysical groups. These also become habits and, from long usage, we come to regard them as integral factors in thought and action. A man has a bad habit when he uses a formula for a crutch in his daily thinking.

7th: OCCULT DISEASES. Every art and science has its own diseases. Each new discovery which man adds to the subject of learning brings with it the possibility of abuse and a new chain of fatal consequences. There are a number of ailments which arise directly from the mis-use of metaphysical science and it is necessary to treat of these separately and at some length.

Type A: comprises such ills as arising from misdirected efforts at spiritual development. The most common form is that caused by attempts to develop the latent spiritual forces through Oriental breathing exercises, concentrations, meditations, the Recitation of mantrams and the stimulation of unnatural mental attitudes. There are great numbers of so-called teachers of metaphysics who teach "short cuts to cosmic consciousness." Practically all of these systems are fatal to the student if he practices them with sufficient industry. Most dabblers are preserved from great harm, however, because they have not the concentration or continuity to perform these exercises for any length of time. The student of metaphysics who attempts any occult practices without previously passing through many years of preparatory probationship and disciplines may expect to ruin his health and endanger his sanity. Efforts to open the CHAKRAS or raise KUNDALINI, or stimulate clairvoyance are followed by nervous break-downs, cerebro congestion, glandular derangements and numerous other ills, some of which are incurable. The only way to treat such diseases successfully is to get the case early, insist upon the patient discontinuing all metaphysical speculation, readjust the diet, stressing physical culture, and surrounding him with simple, normal interests until nature has a chance to build back some of the disintegrated etheric structure.

Type B: arises usually out of spiritism, mediumship and efforts to develop clairvoyant powers through a formula generally known as "going into the silence." To sit in a dark room thinking about nothing is an almost open invitation to obsession. By the word "obsession" the occult philosophers understood: the superimposition of one personality over another. In modern medicine, the patient is usually classed with the insane. Obsession may be of three kinds:

That in which a discarnate entity, once human, attaches itself to the invisible bodies of a living person. A discarnate entity which will do this is usually of a low type and its attachment to the living person is for the gratification of appetite and desire. Such obsessions may be continual or intermittent. When continual, the person obsessed generally manifests destructive and degenerate tendencies and often completely loses their own identity. In intermittent cases, the sufferer has temporary lapses into lucidity.

The second general form of obsession is when the patient is over-shadowed or dominated by an invisible entity, not human, an elementary or elemental spirit. This form of obsession reduces the sufferer to a completely irrational state. The third form in which the unfortunate truth seeker comes under the domination of a person, not dead, but who uses the negative organism of the obsessed person for the accomplishment of some special purpose, usually nefarious. The only way to work with cases of obsession is by definite occult methods. Very often, the physician has to force the obsessing entity out of the body of the patient through a tremendous exertion of will power, and if he is not properly equipped for his task, the physician may become a victim of the obsession himself. The problem of obsession is treated in the New Testament under the terminology of "casting out demons!"

Type C: In addition to these major forms of occult disease there are numerous others which have been cataloged by Paracelsus, but we need here only sum them up under the general heading of occult mal-practice, or as it is more commonly known, black magic. It is an eternal but unwritten law of the philosophers that no secret of occult philosophy can be used legitimately for any selfish or personal reason. It is said of the Initiate as of Jesus that; others he can help but himself he cannot save. By this it is not meant that each person should not protect himself by every reasonable and proper means, but he must never attempt to direct occult forces upon himself. Those who study metaphysics therefore with an eye to the improvement of their material state and in order that they may have an advantage over their fellow creatures and more readily exploit them, are guilty of the unpardonable sin. Spiritual arts must always be used for the common good and any other application is deadly. Selfishness disqualifies a metaphysician and if he enters upon the subject of metaphysics with an ulterior motive that motive itself will be his undoing. The shores of the sea of metaphysics are strewn with the wreckage of the unworthy.

We can only have true contentment when we live in perfect harmony with the law which created us and by which we are maintained. Any deviation from this law brings about our destruction. Absolute adjustment with Nature's purposes is the secret of both happiness and longevity. Disease is a departure from Nature; health a return again. To realize this is to possess the secret of life and to apply this realization is to live. Nature is just and the unjust must perish for their intemperance; Nature is impersonal and all that is personal must pass away. Nature envies nothing, is jealous of nothing, and is a stranger to ambition. All who are motivated by impulses less universal than those of life itself will be destroyed by the inadequacy of their own ideals. Those who are narrow cease for lack of breadth; those who are shallow perish for lack of depth. Only such as are in all things moderate, in all things consistent, and in all things natural can survive, for these live on because they partake of the qualities of continuance. Sharing in the qualities of the gods who have neither beginning nor ending man thus unfolds one by one every divine potentiality until his divine destiny is at length fulfilled. Disease, decay, and death are absorbed into the effulgency of the illumined soul; and man diverging from the limitations of the flesh, inclines towards immortality, to finally merge himself with infinite and changeless Good.

THE END

WE WOULD APPRECIATE YOUR COOPERATION IN KEEPING YOUR CORRECT ADDRESS ON FILE IN OUR OFFICE TO THE END THAT WE MAY BE SPARED THE EXTRA EXPENSE OF RE-MAILING AND YOU WILL GET YOUR LETTER PROMPTLY.

A SUGGESTION-----BOOKS FROM THE PEN OF MANLY P. HALL MAKE EXCELLENT CHRISTMAS GIFTS FOR YOUR FRIENDS. WRITE FOR OUR FREE CATALOGUE.

DECEMBER 1, 1934

Dear Friend,

In our last letter, we examined the subject of Ethics in an effort to discover the nature of good. This month we must seek that cause in man, which was defined by the ancients as the "fountain of ever-flowing good." Psychology is the fourth department of philosophy, and comprehends the entire field of what is now called mental phenomena. The word psychology actually means: the voice, language, or science of the soul. But this original meaning is now, for the most part disregarded, and a new definition has been formulated which limits psychology to the consideration and analysis of the mind and its reflexes.

When a department of learning passes from a theoretical to a so-called practical state, it is said to cease to be an art and becomes a science. The modern psychologist, therefore, regards himself as a scientist rather than a philosopher. It is very questionable, however, whether psychology will ever be as useful as a science as it would be if it were perfected as a philosophy. The virtue of science lies in the intensity of its penetration. The virtue of philosophy lies in the breadth of its viewpoint.

Mystical and metaphysical psychology was developed in India and Egypt and finds its most perfect expression in the transcendentalism of Plato and Proclus. After the decadence of Classical learning, mystical psychology continued as an aspect of Christian metaphysics. During the Middle Ages it dominated Christian viewpoint. This branch of learning was particularly cultivated by the medieval Rosicrucians. Among its ablest exponents were Paracelsus, Jacob Bohme and Robert Fludd. By the beginning of the 18th century, metaphysical speculations were declining in the face of the scientific viewpoint. The "physical" universe was discovered. The ancients viewed the material world as impermanent and comparatively unimportant. They took the attitude that man's spiritual existence was eternal and his material existence only a matter of three or fourscore years. Consequently, they wasted little time on man's temporal state.

In the beginning of the 19th century, all this was changed. Man's spiritual perpetuation was turned over to the tender peeping of a static theology, and his physical life became the sole object of so-called exact learning. This eclipse of mysticism produced an unbalanced viewpoint, which deprived a great part of humanity of a balanced concept of life. By the middle of the 19th century metaphysical organizations began to appear. The memberships of these groups were largely made up of conscientious objectors revolting against the insufficiency of material science as a substitute for philosophy and mysticism.

By the beginning of the 20th century, metaphysicians had become more or less a class apart. The majority of nominally educated and civilized people were hopelessly enmeshed in efficiency and prosperity complexes. Since the economic collapse of 1929 the interest in philosophy in all of its branches has greatly increased, and before the end of the present century we may expect a renaissance of metaphysical psychology.

We may therefore formulate two definitions of psychology to distinguish the two methods of approach—ancient and modern. Ancient psychology sought to examine soul as the medium between spirit and body. Modern psychology, accepting the mind as the origin of man's rational and reasonable existence, seeks to analyze and classify its processes and consequences.

Ancient psychology derives its authority directly from metaphysics; modern psychology from physics.

Mystical psychology may be outlined as follows:

The universe in its three parts manifests the triune nature of that Divine Essence from which all beings have their origin; by which they are sustained; and into which they are finally merged. According to Aristotle, all intelligent men honor God after the number of 3, by natural instinct. The three qualifications of the Divine constitution are termed "worlds," and together make up the Macrocosm or universal wholeness. According to the Rosicrucians, the three parts of the World are as follows:

1. The Imperial Heaven, the eternal and unchanging spiritual essence, the source and support of all life.

2. The Starry or Ethereal Region, which is emanated from the Imperial Heaven and was termed by the Chaldeans the Second or Administering Cause.

3. The Elementary Region; the sphere of effects, the formal world which receives into itself the impulses of the Ethereal diffusion.

Robert Fludd declares the number 3 to represent the Imperial Root; the square of this number, the 9, the Ethereal diffusion; and the cube of 3, 27 the Elementary essences. These numbers, if added together: 27 plus 9 plus 3: equal 39; which, if cabalistically again added, equal 12. Twelve represents the Zodiac of celestial causes. The 1 and the 2 is again added, revealing Aristotle's Divine Root, the 3, and the cycle returns to its own source.

The three regions or conditions of Divinity—divine, ethereal and elementary—are equivalent to the familiar terms; spirit, soul and body. Thus, SOUL corresponds to the Ethereal diffusion or sphere of secondary causes. As in the universe, so in man. The soul represents the medium binding man as a spiritual essence to man as a material body.

The Platonists called the soul "that general virtue which engenders and preserves all things," and in this definition Virgil also concurs. The alchemists referred to it as the "bond of the elements!" The spirit supports the soul, and the soul supports the body. The soul is always regarded as a vast organism, containing within itself the source of all productiveness. Hermes infers this thought in his celebrated definition: "The world (soul) is the son of God, and man is the son of the world."

Ancient psychology, in consequence of this background, regarded the soul as a sensitive mirror in which the whole universe is reflected. The soul binds the individual personality to the heavens, the stars and the planets. Disposition and temperament have their origin in the patterns which are set up in the soul by action and interaction of celestial and sidereal forces. The soul impinges itself upon the body through seven vital centers and seven essential processes. Some of the ancients went so far as to consider the soul of the individual as a complete super-human entity. This is the Anthropos, the over-soul of Emerson, the god or daemon of Socrates, and the one-eyed Cyclops of Homer. The Alexandrian mystics, accepting the soul as a Messianic individuality, considered a union of the personality with its soul as the philosophical marriage. The same thought is contained in the Apocalypse of St. John, a writing undoubtedly inspired by Gnostic and Hermetic speculation. Here, the soul is referred to as the bridegroom; and again, as the lamb; the Holy City, Jerusalem, which symbolizes the material body, is lifted up by regeneration to become the bride of the lamb, or to be reunited forever with its own over-soul.

Pythagoras represented the soul by the ogdoad, or the number 8. According to him, it possessed eight powers or attributes of which seven pertain to sense and cognition, and the eighth to generation or reproduction. These eight represent the seven planets and the earth. A secret is contained within this arrangement, for by it, the physical body of man is viewed as the last or eighth extension of the soul.

In the Mithraic rites of the Persians, the soul is represented by a ladder of seven rungs, its upper end resting upon the spiritual nature and its lower end supported by the material world.

The mental processes, which are now the sole concern of psychology, were only one of the numerous manifestations of soul-power in the ancient system of psychology. The soul was not only the origin of thought, but was the source of all manifestations of consciousness, from contemplation to imagination. The body itself, physically considered, was merely a mechanical instrument, possessing neither perceptive nor reflective power. It is true that the body impulse which motivates and enlightens it originates in the soul. The experience which arises from action is recorded, not in the body, but in the soul itself. Evolution should therefore be regarded not as the growing of bodies, or the unfoldment and development of bodies, but rather as soul growing up through bodies. It is the soul which knows and remembers; it is the soul which bestows wisdom upon the body, out of experiences. At death, the soul deserts the body, carrying away to its own essence all of the records of physical action.

The purpose of ancient psychology was, therefore, to attempt by philosophical processes to distinguish the proper constitution of the soul itself and to view it with the mind's eye in its separate aspects. The differentiation of the soul-entity and its culture by philosophic discipline was the true and original field of psychology. Wise men, realizing that the flesh is weak and impermanent, invested as little as possible in the corporeal fabric. They sought rather to strengthen the soul's dominion over the body. They desired to so simplify bodily processes and mortal concerns that the soul had a maximum of freedom. Socrates believed that in the unregenerate man, the soul was mixed with the bodily principles. A Socratic illustration may be used:

Considering the body as earth and the soul as water, the confusion of them results in mud or slime. Thus, the constitution of the unenlightened or uninitiated person was said to be murky or muddy. If, however, these elements are allowed to remain quiet for a certain length of time, they will separate. The mud and heavier particles will sink to the bottom, leaving the water upon the top comparatively clear. If, however, you agitate these elements, they will again become confused. The irrational impulses of the animal man are consequently constantly riling and confusing the soul and body, but peace and tranquility of the wise allows the lower or bodily elements to settle to their own estate and the soul become clear.

Let us now compare this older concept of psychology with modern opinions on the subject. The term "mind" is now used to designate man's subjective, rational part. All processes not admittedly physical are presumed to be mental. The psychologist of the modern school does acknowledge a mental nature, not necessarily identical with the brain structure, nor resulting merely from the automatic activities of the brain. As to the exact nature of "mind," definitions are hazy. In fact, modern psychology is better equipped to classify mental activities than it is to define the nature of the mind itself. Following the natural impulse described by Aristotle, the mind is psychologically considered as a threefold structure even by the moderns.

Where facts are lacking, opinions are usually numerous and contradictory. The several schools of modern psychology and psychological philosophy can scarcely be regarded as in agreement, and it would be almost impossible to find a common denominator for their conclusions. There is some agreement, however, upon the division of the mind into conscious, subconscious, and unconscious parts. Professor James of Harvard, probably the most famous psychologist of the modern school, was once asked for a definition of the subconscious mind. He declined to give a definition on the ground that he had not yet discovered a satisfactory definition for the conscious mind. The opinion seems to be that the conscious mind is a term applicable to that department of mental processes, which is direct and evident. The surface of the intellect includes the field of phenomena in which the thoughts are consistent with evident facts and arise from adequate and evident causes. For example: Mr. A. has a mental antipathy to Mr. B. Some time ago Mr. B. cheated Mr. A. in business, therefore there is an evident, natural and reasonable origin for Mr. A's attitude. Another example: a young person spends twenty years in school; later in life, he demonstrates certain knowledge which is traceable to his schooling; Thus, in the thinking process, the cause is equal to the effect, and there is no particular mystery in the relationship of ideas.

The second department of the mind is termed the subconscious. The subconscious mind is a field of obscure mental processes. The relationship between mental cause and effect is either distorted or obscured. Psychology acknowledges that there must be a cause for every effect, but mental refraction of ideas may disarrange the process of mental patterns. The factor of intensity appears. Two people respond to a similar thought with differing degrees of intensity, according to the chemistry of temperament. Mental complexes are "scars" in the subconscious mind. Complexes distort and disproportion the values of ideas and are the most common causes of personal idiosyncrasies. The field of the subconscious mind lies behind the sphere of the conscious mental processes, contributing attitudes. For example: Mr. A. does not like Mr. B. Mr. B. has never injured Mr. A. therefore the attitude is unexplainable without recourse to psychoanalysis. Or again, a person suffers throughout life from an inferiority complex, which renders him incapable of normal social intercourse with others. The cause for such a condition may be traced to some comparatively insignificant incident in childhood, which has been distorted out of all proportions by the subconscious processes of the mind.

The third department of the mind, which is termed the unconscious, is regarded as the abstract causal sphere of the mind. It contains no thoughts, but is rather the reservoir of mental energies from which an active mental energy or virtue is constantly flowing into the subconscious and conscious parts of the mind. This sphere of pure mind defies anything that even approaches analysis, but is acknowledged as a hypothetical necessity in that all energies must have a source and all complexity must arise from essentially simple elements.

Upon the principles of psychology as now formulated, two more or less practical sciences have been established: psychoanalysis and psychotherapy. Psychoanalysis, which in turn includes several more specialized fields, seeks to discover the keynote of individual consciousness by analyzing the conscious processes and the subconscious complexes of the individual. The theory is pragmatic. Pragmatism assumes that the intrinsic nature of any force may be discovered by the consequences emanating from that force. This is modern cabalism. The ancient Jewish mystics declared that the substance of Divinity could never be examined, but that God could be discovered through his works. In the same way, the rational man may never be examined by scientific processes, but its qualities may be approximated by an analysis of impulses, emotions, thoughts and attitudes.

Human beings group themselves into two general classes: introverts and extroverts. In the extrovert, impulse and action are closely related and inhibitions and complexes are few. With the introvert, repression is the dominant keynote. Repression is closely allied to complexes; the introvert is generally a victim of tangled and distorted impulses which have found no outlet or expression through the conscious mental processes.

Psychotherapy is based upon the evident and undeniable premise that disorders in the mental life are bound to produce disastrous physical reflexes. Grief will break down cell structure; anger will decrease vitality; worry will prevent the knitting of bones; and a life which is victimized by mental irascibilities is bound to be physically inefficient. Many diseases are at least perpetuated by wrong thinking. In nearly all forms of sickness, recovery is retarded by psychological inhibitions. Normalcy of thinking is a virtue greatly to be desired. The average person is less able to diagnose his mental ailments than he is to diagnose physical infirmities, which may afflict him. We live with our own thoughts so long that we grow accustomed to them, no matter how bad they may be. Psychotherapy seeks to extend the life of man and enlarge his sphere of usefulness by putting the mind in order, and freeing the intellect of its biases and its false viewpoints.

Very truly yours,

Manly P Hall

944 West 20th Street.
Los Angeles, Calif.

THE MASTERY OF FEAR - I

This lecture was given by Mr. Hall at the world CONGRESS OF RELIGIONS, AT THE CENTURY OF PROGRESS EXPOSITION, CHICAGO, 1933.

The true purpose of civilization is to ensure the security of man, individual and collective. We must measure progress in terms of human security. We must regard as progressive every contribution to security and we must regard as retrogressive every action or measure which hazards this security. Aboriginal mankind dwelt in a condition of physical and spiritual insecurity. Ignorance and superstition impoverished his courage, leaving him a victim of countless fears and terrors. There was evil in the lightning and disaster rode upon the wings of the storm. Primitive man feared nature, but modern man fears man. With education, we have dispelled the tribal ghosts of ancient days; we have laid low the demons which haunted the aboriginal world; with medical science, we have combatted the plagues with engineering feats we have turned the floods. The prodigious effort of evolving man has reaped its reward in terms of increasing human security. With our present knowledge, and with reasonable anticipation of further development in the several fields of learning, we may say with confidence that within the next five hundred years man will have so mastered the elements, which previously so offended him, that life will cease to be hazardous, and with reasonable precaution the majority of mankind can survive triumphantly the ordinary vicissitudes of nature.

Along the shore of Lake Michigan, unfolds the panorama of Chicago's Century of Progress. This great Exposition is dedicated primarily to the glorification of the intensive mechanistic productiveness of the last hundred years. Numerous grotesquely shaped buildings house fantastic arrays of devices and improvements, adjutants, etc., by the development and use of which our civilization has come to what it is today. We should be justly proud of the ingenuity by which these mechanistic miracles have come to pass, but at the same time it is not amiss to question certain unemphasized aspects of what we please to term progress.

Where in all this Exposition is to be found exhibited one single evidence of ethical, moral or aesthetic progress? Where is the proof that the humanity of today is happier, wiser, or intrinsically better, than the humanity of a hundred years ago? Where are the proofs of increasing individual or collective security? In other words, where is the evidence of real CIVILIZATION in this Century of Progress?

True, we have added greatly to our conveniences, multiplied our industries, compounded our economics and heaped up fortunes that even Croesus might have envied. But where is brotherhood, where is well-founded faith, where is vision, and where that fraternity of effort and ideal without which all so-called progress is but an illusion?

> "There is only one ambition that is good, and that is: so, to live NOW that none may weary of life's emptiness, and none may have to do the task we leave undone!" - Tsiang Samdup

Strange creatures from strange parts have been brought to this Fair to edify gaping tourists from the outlying districts, yet nowhere on exhibition in this Century of Progress is to be found a happy man, a wise man, or one who can face the future with security and understanding. We wonder if what we call a Century of Progress has not really been a century of complications, in which all simple and direct values have been lost sight of. We live lives on tangents in environments of complexity.

All true progress must be measured in the wellbeing of man, and in its ruthless course of exploitation industry is not only indifferent to man's wellbeing, but has reduced him to an insignificant and almost unnecessary factor in the onward rumble of an economic empire.

As we study into the motives of men, as these motives are objectified in their cultural systems, it becomes increasingly evident that civilization is only an appearance, a shallow surfacing beneath which still rage the aboriginal emotions of the prehistoric world. We are haunted by the sinister ghosts of our past selves. We would be kind, but there is cruelty in our blood; we would be honest, but there is craftiness in our marrow. On our lips are words of forgiveness, but our souls mumble to the ancient law. An eye for an eye, and a tooth for a tooth.

We must be forgiven then if we fear our fellowman a little, we must be excused if we reason in our hearts that he is no better than ourselves. If we behold beneath the fair aspect of this great civilization a cold, glittering cruelty, we have just reason for some apprehension. We know that, all to the contrary notwithstanding, with a few exceptions, mankind is not civilized. He has grown skillful, but he has not grown good; he has grown old, but he has not grown up; he has grown wealthy, but he has not grown generous; he has grown powerful, but he has not grown kind; he has gained knowledge, but he has not grown wise.

Our modern civilization is ruled by the law of the jungle—the survival of the fittest—spoils to the strong, misery to the weak. At the end of the ages stands TODAY, and in the today stands man's great economic empire; an empire dominated by ignorance, superstition and fear, where nothing is secure, where no one is safe, where virtue, honesty and truth are words, and where treasons, stratagems and spoils ravish the earth. When a man shudders today and says, "I am afraid," his is not a blind and senseless terror of some benighted Bushman; his is a well-grounded fear, a fear of things seen and known, not of ghosts. Civilization has weakened man and left him a victim of luxury; civilization has deprived man of resourcefulness, snuffed out his sense of individual sufficiency, and left him an absolute weakling dependent utterly upon the commodities and luxuries of his social plan. The average man can no longer build his own house, kill his own game, weave his own cloth, defend his own hearth, nor gaze out at life with some realization of his personal strength. No matter how rich or how poor he may be today, he is a slave, a serf, utterly dependent upon things and things and things. His security is not in his own keeping. He depends almost entirely upon factors beyond his control, and as his fortunes ebb and flow, he must sit impotently by and hope and fear.

The civilized man is a civilization addict. He is doped with our modern industrial psychology. He knows that he is miserable, that there is no probability of his ever being anything else, yet he will fight to defend the very evils which destroy him. He is afraid, and he obeys unquestioningly the despotic edicts of his fear masters. Millions of men and women, living, working, dying—always afraid. Afraid to live, afraid to think, afraid to speak, yes, even afraid to hope. The proletarians of the world are afraid of their jobs, living in constant terror that the next payday will be the last. Mothers and fathers are afraid for their children. The old, in which both fear and hope are dead, and the young in which hope and fear are strong. Men might learn to love one another a little if they did not have to fear one another so much. But where fear is love cannot be, for terror cannot dwell with understanding. Those who have fear, lest they shall lose; those who have not, fear lest they shall not gain. The great fear for their lives, and the humble are afraid of the great. Nations are afraid of one another's armaments. Great nations are hated for their power and little nations are envied even for the little which they do possess. Each year, an all-fearing world spends billions in armaments. The nations of today live by Napoleons code that God is on the side of the heaviest artillery. A hundred civilized nations plotting war, scheming schemes of wealth, cheating and conniving, stealing and plundering by a code that forgives the victor all his sins and exterminates the vanquished.

Fear is not all an illusion then, although the things men fear are for the most part unreal. Fear was bred in the swamps and fens of the first jungle. Terror roamed the primordial wild and though ages have passed and many changes have come to this old world, fear still comes with the night and terror lurks in the smoke of industry.

While men warred and pillaged upon the earth, their gods warred and pillaged in the heavens. Theology was once, but the instituted tyranny of the invisible. The priests of old used fear as an instrument to control their wandering and nomadic peoples, and if man has grown virtuous, it is only fair to say that in some cases he was frightened out of his vices. There are many law-abiding men and women to every virtuous one, for laws were made to keep us from destroying ourselves. In the course of several millenniums, the religions of the world became greatly complicated. The medicine man and the witch-doctor were gradually metamorphosed into the clergy.

Sects and creeds divided, over painfully insignificant issues, until through little understanding humanity had the burden of ecclesiastical dissension added to its already heavy burden of woes. Religions, like humanity itself, had so many things in common and so few differences; and yet, like humanity, they ignored these many things in common and so magnified the few differences that theology became a ghastly travesty of religion. Nearly three hundred sects of Christianity alone have remembered the Fatherhood of God, but forgotten the Brotherhood of Man. So, faith, which should have multiplied human certainties, has for the most part only increased its fears.

At this time, we are gathered here in a Fellowship of Faiths. We come here, as friends, from far thoughts and distant places. We are here because we believe that the beliefs and ideals of the race are so intrinsically identical that they greatly overbalance any small differences which may seem to exist. We are of several races and a score of nations. As races, we have persecuted one another, as nations we have warred against one another; each has feared and hated the other and yet in this assembly the evident sincerity of purpose and the overwhelming humanity which is the motive for this assemblage binds us together far more closely than any other differences may separate us. But unfortunately, we gather here not as nations or as races, but, if the matter be sincerely stated, as individuals. We are really expressing personal convictions, or at the most convictions of small groups existing within greater bodies of peoples which do not possess similar convictions. Let us face the fact truthfully. The various religious doctrines of the world are not liberal; they are creed-bound and heavy with fear. But through each of these creeds there rise isolated individuals who, having come to sense the more real values of life, interpret into their creeds a broadness which is really their own.

It is far from desirable that the various religions of the world should give up their own identities to be merged into some common indefiniteness, which is neither understandable nor acceptable to the numerous followers. It is, however, just and reasonable, and well within the province of religious premise, that the numerous sects which unite in the adoration of the common Father should occasionally unite on earth for the more practical purpose of furthering that Father's work among the peoples, of the world. The majority of the inhabitants of the earth are nominally addicted to some religion, and the majority of the inhabitants of the earth show little evidence of any application of their religious addictions. If perchance we were to examine the great evils which have descended upon the earth, we should discover that most of them arise among nominally religious people, are perpetuated by nominally religious people, with small glory to God and less good to man.

FROM THE WEAKNESS OF WORDS, WE MUST RISE TO THE STRENGTH OF ACTION. Religion has failed as long as man must remain afraid of man. The men we fear are seldom infidels; they are of our own faiths and beliefs. THEY PRAY BESIDE US ON SUNDAY AND THEY PREY UPON US ON MONDAY. The purpose of religion is not only to convince one man that there is a God within his brother; it is necessary that the brother himself be sufficiently convinced of this indwelling divinity that his relationship with other men may be tinctured by this belief.

At the end of this Congress of Religions, we shall each go again our own way, some returning to distant lands, most of us to continue some ministry of spiritual or philosophical education. Within a twelvemonth, some of the nations may be at war and your peoples will be praying to the god of armies for victory. You return as sheep among wolves, you go to serve a world which does not understand brotherhood or love or peace. There is not one among us who dares to hope that in our short years the evils which infect the race may be removed. In all ages, prophets and patriarchs of heroic vision have taught and loved, suffered and died in the service of an unbelieving world. Yet all of these great teachers, and the faiths which they have established, are agreed in one thing, that the Universal Bather, by whatsoever name He may be known, is ever watchful over the destiny of His creation. There is law in the universe and according to the law, all creatures must work out their own salvations with diligence.

The last few years have witnessed the collapse of man's industrial-economic civilization. A cultural system built up in defiance of all spiritual and ethical law has demonstrated its inadequacy and unfitness to survive. This emergency is religion's opportunity. This is no time for jarring sects and little isms seeking grandeur. This is a supreme opportunity for the idealists of the world to turn from their contentions over pots and tittles and unite in practical spiritual service, and practical religious education. The first task which confronts us is the consolidation of our own fraternity. If the leaders cannot be united, the followers cannot be brought together. Remember, this would not be an absorption of religions, but a brotherhood of religions. If each faith sincerely rejoices in the good works of other faiths with a camaraderie of purpose, it will lay the foundation for a better civilization to come.

If the religions of the world fail to rise to this great emergency in the soul experience of the race, it is unlikely that organized theology will survive the present century. Either spiritual idealism must rescue the race or else vanish away with the civilization which it has failed.

The first step in the re-education of man must be the reframing of the code of human values. The Rule of Gold must give place to the Golden Rule. Men must be taught that true wealth is only possible when society is functioning on a spiritual and not a physical foundation. Wealth is not a matter of money. True wealth is measured in terms of wisdom, peace, happiness, and well-being. Ambition is the deadly enemy of well-being and causes man to live in constant apprehension, hazard, and uncertainty. It forces him inevitably along a course of destructive procedure which can end only in disaster and death.

If twenty-five percent of the religious people of the world would LIVE their religion, heaven would exist right here on earth. The question must naturally arise: How can a person actually belong to a religious body and in no matter of importance act consistently with the doctrines of that body? This is a real problem for theologians. Is it possible that theology has failed to throw proper emphasis upon the APPLICATION of spiritual principles to terrestrial affairs? Have the various religions demanded certain standards of living from their members? In this age of success, just closed, we all grew a little lax.

(To be continued)

NOTICE

YOU may be glad to know that we have reprinted several of the small booklets that have been out of print for a number of years. We can now supply you, The Noble Eightfold Path—Melchizedek, and the mystery of Fire—The Mystery of Electricity—Right Thinking the Royal Road to Health—The Culture of the Mind. These booklets sell for 35 cts each or 3 for $1.00. Please add sales tax in Calif.

JANUARY 1, 1935

Dear Friend,

DURING the last few years, a great wave of mysticism has swept over the world. The heart of mankind is hungry for greater knowledge, the soul yearning for fuller understanding, has sought to tear away the veil which forever drapes the figure of Wisdom. Man has sought to learn those mystic truths so long lost to the world, and in his study and search he has found that there are strange and mysterious beings known to the world as Initiates. Among the ancient works and the mystery schools of those peoples now dead, strange ceremonies called initiations were given in some mysterious way and the popular mind has come to believe that there is a mystic rite, an initiative ceremonial, which makes man one with the immortals, and in the name of this wonderful and mystic concept terrible crimes have been committed against the spiritual and occult teachings. There is probably no word in the English language that has been so abused, so misused, so often used and so little understood, as the word "Initiation!" Every dream, every phantom form, every unusual happening, has been called the initiation and all over the world temples have sprung up in the name of the Mystery Schools to initiate candidates into the Wisdom teachings, some of them without cost but in the majority of cases a heavy fee accompanies the initiation in which for, say, $25.00 the candidate is dubbed "Sir Somebody" or made a leading luminary in some mystic shrine.

The result of this perversion is that the sacredness, the beauty, and the true realization of the meaning of initiation has been lost to the world, for it is very true that there are none who can so damage a religion or an idea as those who claim to be its followers. How long it will take the world to learn that initiations are not ceremonials it is difficult to say, but sometime each individual must realize that swinging robes and incense burners and other trimmings do not constitute initiation, and that no one on the face of the earth could buy it for the fortune of Croesus nor in any way receive it until he himself by his life has become worthy of its mystic blessing.

There are few in this world who know what real initiation is, and there are fewer still who having discovered it really want to so live that this mystic rite may be unfolded within their souls. The true initiate is a very wondrous and mysterious being and any words that we can say concerning such a one are very poor, indeed. Those who have not already walked the path can have but a feeble idea of what an initiate really is, for such a one has unfolded within himself or herself, as the case may be, certain principles of which the average layman knows nothing.

> To him who truly seeks the Middle Way, the Middle Way will open. One step forward is enough.
>
> - Tsiang Samdup.

The powers of life and death, the powers of destruction and construction, the mystic principles of integration. And disintegration, all these are in the hands of the Great Ones of God. The knowledge of life is the mystic power of the Initiate, for only those who have walked the ways of many can ever know what the laurels of initiation mean. Only when his heart is filled with love for humanity and with the great suffering and great peace of those who know, can he so express the powers within himself that he is of use in so great a plan. The Initiate has the mindless mind of spirit which thinks only the thoughts of life, to the source of which he each day draws nearer; he is filled with the understanding of nature's plan for her children and only this knowledge holds in check a heart that would otherwise break with sorrow. He knows that strange, sweet melancholy, that mystic feeling few have ever realized, such as must have filled the soul of Jesus as He wept over Jerusalem. The true initiate is initiated by God and not by man and he will give his life, his soul, his very being, to lift suffering in the name of the Father.

It is only those who have a heart great enough to enfold all creation, a consciousness as great and broad as life itself, who are even on the road to initiation, those who's very being is a mirror of the Divine, whose every thought is to save, whose every power is expanded to raise, whose every action is a blessing, who reach out with hands ever stronger to aid suffering humanity. Those and those alone know the true meaning of initiation. Those whose eyes have never seen suffering, those whose hearts have never been broken, those who are tied by earthly ambitions, can never receive that celestial influx of life which comes to those who have prepared their vehicles in the way of the law and the great love.

The Initiate is slowly reaching out into the Great Unknown, lighting each corner of chaos with his own glory, bathing all life in the warmth of his own soul, limited only by his own unfoldment. On through the ages he is dispelling ignorance and darkness by the ever-broadening sphere of his own light. It is those who have dedicated their lives and being to feed the flame of the Eternal One that its light may shine more brightly whom we call the Initiates and, oh, how few they are! How few have given up the kingdoms of the earth! How few are ready to give up earthly desires to walk the path that leads to Divinity, holding out the little alms-dish of the Buddha for the words of wisdom and love that are given to those who seek for help that they in turn may serve. To those who seek it in any other way than this, initiation is only a terrible demon. The student may gain growth, the wisdom or so-called power of the Adept may come to him, but still if selfishness is his motive he is cursed to suffer and to go without the things of this world as well as the other, for he is cursed with knowledge, and knowledge brings with it a weight that few shoulders are strong enough to bear.

It is only when that mystic thing comes, the strange, spiritual power of initiation, that to man is given the strength to carry knowledge in the way of light. There are only a few who are ready to take up the cross and follow in the footsteps of those who have consecrated their lives to their fellowmen. There are only a few with strength enough to see the veil of the future lifted and remain sane. There are few who could see the veil of their own destiny raised and still have strength enough to walk the way, and even to those who can stand this great light there comes the still greater test of standing alone in the high places of the world without even the staff of comradeship, for the initiate is ever alone but when truly ordained of the spirit is never lonely.

For with this knowledge that no tongue can speak, no coin of man can buy, there comes something else, a still whisper, the word of eternal life that passes eternally through the soul of the saved. While the Initiate sees the bleeding hearts of his fellowman and the breaking and tearing of living things, he still sees the eternal justice of all things, to him there comes the realization that all is working for good. He sees the divine hand working through the apparent chaos of things and that behind the human discord, there is the divine reason.

Can we face this Great Unknown as the Great Ones have faced it? Can we pass through with the glorious vision of Nirvana forever before us? If we can, we are on the path upward that leads to the feet of the Great Ones who look down on man with never-changing eyes of love. Very few are there in the world today who are ready to make the great renunciation which the world kotows as initiation.

There comes a time to every soul when there is a parting of the ways, and there are few who will take the stony path, give up the kingdoms of earth, and ascend the rocky crags to the feet of the Liberator. Those who take that path are the true essence of the life we live. Eventually, all will take the path as the light dawns upon them.

If we would take that silent way, we must renounce the selfishness of materiality and slowly and painfully meet bravely the buffets of the world and go on and on in the endless paths that leads into the Unknown. It is those who have done this, sacrificing all without a murmur, whom we know as the Initiates, and we owe them respect and love for they are in truth our Elder Brothers who have gone a little ways before, that they may come back and show us the path to tread.

A time comes when each soul, after having passed the first degrees of initiation, receives the greatest test of all. It is when he reaches the veil that divides him from the world. Nirvana with all its blessings, shines before him while those wandering in the wilderness cry out for help from the darkness below. He stands at the parting of the ways—which path will he choose? The path of initiation is forever the path of sacrifice. No glory, no power, just a selfless willingness to serve the highest. In the robes of the mendicant, the Initiate returns to wander the earth and serve others. While they are apparently imperfect and torn and slandered by the world, yet the hosts of heaven look down and bless them. Those who give up all, even the paradise well-earned and the rest that is theirs, and come back to walk in the muck and mire,—they are the Initiates. It is at that moment the Star of Bethlehem shines out to tell that another Son of God is born among men.

There are many on earth who have made this great renunciation. They have given up peace to walk the streets in rags, to be laughed at and ridiculed, to teach the few who would listen. They have gained great knowledge and great intellect but still they live and speak of simple things. We only see them occasionally and we say that these great ones have been blessed but we do not know the price that they have paid, how they have bathed their souls in tears, how they have been garbed only in their own blood and crucified by their own disciples. This is the price of initiation and it is through these things great souls are born.

We have grown to think that there is only one Son of God but we are all his children, and when one really takes the path that leads to Light, the voice of the Father speaks spiritually within his soul, saying, "This is my Beloved Son in whom I am well pleased." It is only then that the candidate climbs the steps that lead to immortality.

It is sad to think how few who seek the powers of the masters are willing to pay for them with love and thought. With a few paltry dollars and a few fine robes, they honestly believe they can receive that for which Gods have died, which great souls have been crucified to attain and martyrs met their death in the arena. It is a pitiful thing, man's concept of the road to God. "It is sharper than a serpent's tooth to have a thankless child," and how many of them the gods have today!

What is the path that leads to the Initiates? It is the lifting of consciousness through this strange drama, which we call life. Along the great road, all beings are plodding slowly, old and young alike, all walking the same path, the road that leads to the feet of the Masters. There are many shrines along the way, many religions, many creeds, many little chapels where the seeker stops to pray and the weary to rest. But ever onward, all must go until they reach the temple on the top of the lofty crags. In daily life, we have our tests; the thought comes to our mind that we hate someone, but what have we to hate? Then thoughts of fear haunt us and sorrow bows us down. Then through the ages comes the realization that all things lead to good. Slowly, we gain the great compassion, the great balance, the heart that is free of pain and pleasure. We have the vision of the great Truth and seek to enfold all living things within the cape of our love. When thoughts like these come to the student, he is learning. It is that feeling of glory that brings with it the touch of pain. Everything we do carries with it a great responsibility. Those who wish to wear the robe of the Initiate must be willing to wear it over a broken heart.

With many people their greatest desire is to escape responsibility or to gain the glory of a great reward but so long as these thoughts fill the soul initiation is impossible. Until the aspirant is living the ritual, he can never learn its mystery; until he can see in his own spiritual being the dying Christ on the cross, he can never truly learn of initiation. It is bought with the gold of spirit and service. When he has so lived as to be worthy of it, then comes the Light. In the darkness of his own closet, far from his brother man, in the silence of his own soul the great mystery unfolds.

Thousands of figures gather round him and the Grand Master is there in his robe of Blue and Gold, the teachers of the ages gather round him; he is in the great hall of his own body through which he must pass to enter the inner room. There alone he passes through things no mortal tongue can speak, there he sees the reason for his being; the things that he must do; the greater works he is privileged to accomplish. And having learned much, his new responsibility is likewise great; having seen the work to be done, he can no longer rest but must wander the world like a lost soul to labor in the endless cause. He lives for one brief moment with those things which are eternal and having glimpsed those wondrous beings, service means everything. He must help all living things to find the light that he has found. Just a silent soul alone, unfolding its wondrous mystery to its own being,—that is Initiation.

Having gone through these tests and removed the love of materiality, he is given the privilege of knowing and realizing the true reason for at least part of the Plan. He goes on now, step by step, coming into the powers which were always his, not in heaven but in hell, for the place of the Initiate is not in the worlds above but in the worlds of darkness for he has consecrated his soul to the redemption of man.

We have among us today those who claim to have passed through great initiations, but do their lives show it? Are they willing to work unseen and unknown with the powers that never shine before the eyes of men? Do they work with the humility and simplicity which is the divine expression of the soul? All true Initiates point out the way by their own beings that others may follow the path to which they have dedicated their lives.

Everyone wants to be an Initiate but if they were the sun would soon go out forever from their lives. Like children, man is always wanting something and weeping for it like a child. The soul filled with uncertainty, selfishness, and materiality can never have the strength of purpose and the unity of balance, to carry the burdens of Initiation. It is a blessing, then, that many are not what they want to be. If it were not so, hearts would be broken that have not the strength to mend. If we could be initiated now, it would do us no good, for each true, upward step must be hewn out of the solid rock of experience that each may take the path by removing from his life the personal things that stand between him and that which he seeks. We must take each cruel word and change it into a dove before we send it on its way.

When we go hence to enter into our Father's house, the greatest reward that can come to us is the privilege of laboring there. Not our will, but the Master's should regulate the expression of our life.

If those who seek Initiation today could only know what it really means, they would realize how false their concepts have been. What have we done that we have the right to Join that little throng of God's chosen ones? If we would labor with them, we must take upon our shoulders their burdens and be one of those who are responsible for the lives of men, and when we have raised our consciousness, our lives, our actions and our thoughts to this point, then we are Initiates in spirit and in truth, for the light of God's plan for man shines forth and envelopes us in its glory and its first gleam shining upon our souls show us the end to which all Initiation leads,—a lonely cross upon a hill.

Yours sincerely,
Manly P. Hall

SOME PHILOSOPHICAL FRAGMENTS
THE MASTERY OF FEAR - II
(Continued from Dec. 1934)

Theologians went into real estate rather heavily. Vast edifices stood proxy for piety and various organizations became more interested in the number of their members than they were in the quality thereof. Religion compromised itself, descended from the non-commercial aloofness which was its original estate. The theological mind wandered from the contemplation of the Kingdom of God to the contemplation of the kingdoms of the earth. The humble simplicity of faith, which was its strength, gave place to a gaudy unsatisfying complexity, and mankind lost its spiritual preceptor.

The cry is: Back to simple things, to simple lives, to an almost mendicant existence. Men, tired of the sham and responsibility of unnecessary possessions, are beginning to question the desirability of accumulation. Religion should lead in this pilgrimage Towards simplicity. Ostentation in faith is unbecoming and the pompous pedagogue is relegated to the limbo. Our world is coming to a philosophy of work, and theology should be a religion of works. As soon as man is satisfied with little, as soon as ambition no longer tempts him to excess, as soon as he regains his power of individual sufficiency, so soon he will master fear.

Mahatma Gandhi is a dramatic example of the new world trend toward simplicity. In his own life, this extraordinary man achieves religion in action. This little brown ascetic challenges the involved theologies and policies of the world. He has accomplished within himself the virtues which men have preached for ages and have failed to live even for a day. Gandhi would bring all men together in a true fellowship of intelligent action and spiritually enlightened endeavor. In his realization of the essential values of life Mahatma Gandhi has mastered fear, and would lead his brother creatures from a collapsing structure of doubt to a newer and broader dwelling of certainties. Impersonal love, sincerely applied to the common problems of mankind, cannot fail to bring about, a beautiful and permanent solution.

When religion approaches the social problem not with threats of hell or hope of heaven, but with a simple handclasp of friendship, when the priest is again the shepherd of his flock, then we may hope for the dawn of a more enlightened age. The greatest preaching of Christendom was done to barefoot men along the road to Nazareth; the supreme inspiration of the Buddhist faith came from a shaven-headed mendicant seated on a hillock with no roof but the sky and no altar but the dry earth. Was Islam ever richer than when the Prophet preached the Suras in secret to a faithful few? Religions are not great because of the numbers of their followers, the vastness of their temples, nor the wealth of their orders; they are great only when their doctrine is vitally necessary to men. All this must be re-clarified if faith is once more to lead the march of progress.

The richest civilization that ever existed is bankrupt for ideals. If this Fellowship of Faiths can bring the great religions of the world to the realization of the necessity of forgetting their schisms and their discords, and uniting to the common task of preserving the idealism of the race, it can make the greatest contribution of all modern times to the preservation of society. In the face of this great opportunity, this great responsibility, nothing else can be considered of importance.

While man is so desperately oppressed with an unfair and unreasonable economic theory of living, it is impossible for him to clarify his mind for the understanding of spiritual matters. While it is true that affliction is a great stimulant to thought, the constant pressure of a hopeless financial tyranny destroys the morale of the mass, and if protracted long enough, results in degradation and chaos. It is highly important that man should put his physical world in order before he turns his attention too completely towards spiritual concerns. Some will say that if man will first become spiritual these other things will adjust themselves, but experience has shown that a certain tranquility of environment is essential to the propagation of idealism. While a few may climb by the rocky path of adversity, the many must be led through green pastures. A man who is in constant fear for the necessities of life is not in a position to be philosophically detached. His perspective is certain to be warped by the pressure of circumstances, he is narrowed to a doctrine of utility. A mind filled with worries has little space in it for ideas. The wealthiest and most powerful nation in the world today is worried nigh unto death. In this crisis, we have tested our intelligence and found it wanting. We have tried our psychologists who are supposed to be experts on all complexes, but their solutions are worse than our dilemma. Our college professors are no better. They have lived so long in the narrow environment of memorization that they have been rendered incapable of thinking by the very weight of education. As for our politicians—well, the less said the better. Our scientists, though rather successful in biological research, are poor economists. As most of their funds come from endowment and donation, they are childishly ignorant of practical matters. Our philosophers—but why bring that up? We have none.

So, all in all, when something happens which redly requires thinking, there is no one left in our very cultivated world who is capable of doing it. These groups of impotent intellectuals, et cetera, are not only without solutions, they are without ideas. They pride themselves for the most part upon their lack of vision. There is only one body in society today which even pretends to idealism and that is the religious world.

If this civilization is going to be saved, it will not be saved by budgets or ballots, it will not be saved by psychanalysis or serums. It must be saved by honest, practical idealism, and without this priceless ingredient, all remedies advanced to solve the present world emergency must fail. A practical example of the spiritual factor in material action is the NRA program. The success of the National Reconstruction Act depends entirely upon one metaphysical element—namely, integrity. Our President has put his faith in the honesty of the American people, but where in the whole theory of modern education, sociology or science, is man being educated in honesty? The government issues each year hundreds of bulletins dealing with the planting of corn, the trapping of wild animals, the weaning of infants, et cetera, and yet nowhere does man receive education in integrity, honesty, truth and practical idealism. If our President, like Diogenes, is having difficulty finding his honest man, it is because economics has made such serious inroads into the spiritual life of man that the honest man is failing from the earth.

If this Fellowship of Faiths can dedicate itself to the production of honest men, if it can preserve and perpetuate those great spiritual ideals which promote honesty and truth, it shall earn for itself the undying gratitude of mankind.

Except for men, humanity has very little to fear. We have fairly well tamed the primordial forces, but we have never been able to check human greed. When people complain about this world, they are really not complaining about the world at all—only the people who are in it. The earth is very abundant, a gentle and kindly mother of living things. She has her moods, but science has learned to anticipate many of them and, in time, may curb them all. But man on this little earth has made himself very uncomfortable. With his national spirit, he has hacked continents into small bits and fenced off acreage under various flags. Since his first appearance, man has been precocious and destructive. With uncurbable ambition and insatiable greed, he has prevented the fulfillment of nearly every good which might otherwise have come to him. A certain religious instinct was his one redeeming emotion. A certain veneration by which, through development, he became a patron of art and beauty; and, enfolding philosophy unto itself, he gradually built a somewhat impressive structure, of at least relative truth, in the midst of the desert of its deceiving's. In more recent times the sciences, philosophies and arts all separated from the religious principle, each going its separate way on a program of isolated individualism. Learning thus became sacred and profane. Profane learning became very profane and finally reached the nadir of its profanity in our recent economic orgy.

The day must sometime come when all the arts, sciences, crafts and philosophies must again be united with the sacred sciences to become one undivided body of divine learning. Until all the transactions between men come to be regarded as spiritual, none of the transactions between men can be truly spiritual. Only when men are honest and gentle one with the other can fear cease. When I know that my brother's smile is from his heart and not from the scheming of his mind, I shall no longer fear. There is no fear where honesty rules, there is no fear where integrity is the basis of relationships, there is no fear where kindliness is the integral element in the compound of relationships.

True religion is integrity in action. It is the DOING of honesty, and the working of truth. Religion is that constructive force which is evident in the lives of truly superior men. The seeds of religion were sown with the beginning of the race, and the full flowering of it will come only with the perfection of the race. But as civilization progresses it is essential that the religious impulse shall progress with it, tincturing and enlivening all material accomplishments and rendering them usable in the permanent structure of progress.

When our wealth, our power or our domain, increases more rapidly than our spiritual development, the result is despotism and tyranny. In the last fifty years we have concentrated our entire resource upon physical progress, suffering from the delusion that with the increase of our worldly goods would come security and happiness. We neglected our spiritual lives. Our religions became mere forms and ceased to be vital forces. The result is a purposeless generation. We have things but not knowing how to use them wisely; we have abused them fatally. WE MUST NOW PAUSE IN OUR ECONOMIC DEBACLE TO ALLOW OUR ASPIRATIONS TO CATCH UP TO OUR AMBITIONS.

Have you ever asked yourself, "where is the world going? what is civilization trying to accomplish? what is the actual reason for this terrific pressure of life?" If you ask these questions, you will get no answer. We know not where we go nor why. We are purposeless, drifting on the currents of impulse, laughing today and crying tomorrow, but absolutely without intent or reason. Tomorrow is only a vacuum into which we seek to shift the responsibilities of today. Tomorrow is no longer an opportunity; to most, it is an impending fatality. Tomorrow is pregnant with the reactions of yesterday. We fear tomorrow even as we regret yesterday.

Can you not realize how greatly, how desperately this modern world needs spiritual guidance? Exploited on every hand by dishonesty and selfishness, is it a wonder that man's faith weakens under the strain of long suffering? If ever in the history of civilization we have needed an honest religion, it is now. We cannot fail this afflicted world. We must rise in new strength and with higher resolve, putting aside the small matters over which we have haggled, and rededicate our faiths and ourselves to this supreme human duty.

Fear is man's basic weakness, and it is founded upon ignorance and oppression. Courage is the supreme strength in man and is based upon wisdom and justice. A civilization which is established in fear will perish in fear, but a civilization which is established in the courage of conviction and upon the principles of justice will survive as long as the universe endures. All true progress points towards enlightenment. Enlightenment is the ultimate state of man and enlightenment is wisdom in action. The primitive barbarism in the human soul will ultimately be transmuted into a real and permanent civilization. Ideality must not only uphold this goal; it must point the way to the accomplishment of this end through practical example. The perfection of the race does not imply a final identity of purpose or action hut rather a magnificent cooperation in purpose and action. We look forward to the age in which all men, performing these labors most suitable and desirable to themselves, shall unite in a common admiration for all good worlds.

Religion must point the way in this new era, taking its stand firmly amidst the crumbling ruins of materiality. The spiritual codes of the earth must rescue the vision of the race from the obscurity which threatens it. There is no perfection of the part separate from the perfection of the whole. There is no single department of society which can function smoothly while the rest is in chaos. Man cannot be spiritually normal and at the same time physically disorganized. He must put his whole world in order in a Fellowship of Faith and a coordination of effort. Let us each according to our light, but with sincerity of purpose and honesty of heart, strive to preserve and disseminate those essential truths which are indeed the hope of the world. The End.

A LITTLE ESSAY ON BEAUTY

Beauty is an elusive power, whose presence is an invisible asset, whose absence leaves a supreme need unfulfilled. Beauty has been defined as symmetry, or the harmony of form. It is a proper adjustment of parts, a reasonable synthesis of members, an order pleasing because it is proper.

Beauty is not identical with an object nor with the grouping of objects. It is a spirit which is created by the proper bringing together of a number of parts which may not be necessarily beautiful in themselves but which produce a harmonious whole. Physical beauty is invoked by a consistent co-ordination of elements. We may ask, what is the criterion of consistency and, with Plotinus, we may say that the soul which is the criterion of consistency in man, rejoicing in beholding other natures harmonious to itself, becomes the determinator of beauty. The soul of man is rational. Rationality is simply beauty upon the plane of reason. Thus, the rational soul, beholding other reasonable natures, rejoices in the similarity and hence establishes the criterion of excellence.

In addition to the beauty of form, we have beauty of sound, which is harmony; beauty of mode or tempo, which is rhythm; beauty of morality, which is virtue; beauty of mind, which is intellect; and beauty of spirit, which is the ultimate good.

The Platonic Triad is the One, the Beautiful, and the Good, and the unity or wholeness of the world was erected upon this triangle. The One was the substance of all natures and beings; the Beautiful, the perfection of all natures and beings; and the Good, the utility of all natures and beings.

Without beauty, the soul of the people cannot develop itself properly and sanely. We say that a man must eat in order to live. Not only does he need physical food, but there is a metaphysical nature within him which must be fed with a superior sort of diet. The soul is fed through the eyes and the other sense perceptions. That which is grotesque or distorted is a poison to the soul; for, sensing the asymmetrical figure through the faculties, the soul suffers from the shock of the incongruity. The inner nature feeds upon environment and he who surrounds himself with beauty nourishes his aesthetic nature, without which he must fail as a rational creature.

Beauty is essential to human survival. Deprived of its influence, man speedily deteriorates into a state of crassness and degradation. Plotinus declares the most worthy profession to be the service of the beautiful and that to destroy beauty was the most heinous of all crimes. Greece produced the most beautiful civilization the world has ever known by emphasizing the necessity of aesthetics and establishing beauty as one of the pillars of the state.

One of the great needs of our civilization is a greater emphasis upon aesthetic ideals to modify the extreme utilitarianism of our age and thus permit the survival of the subtler elements of culture.

PARIS, FEBRUARY 1, 1935

Dear Friend:

The fifth department of Philosophy is termed Epistemology, and is devoted to the essential nature of knowledge itself. It is the province of Epistemology to distinguish between absolute and relative truth, and to examine the validity of the premises upon which the assumption of knowledge is based.

The existence of an absolute knowledge to be comprehended by any individual entity is a mooted problem. Man is a partially evolved animal creation, enjoying certain animal extensions of consciousness, but also circumscribed by certain animal limitations of consciousness. The human organism has achieved to no ultimates of refinement, therefore—is it possible for a structure, itself greatly limited, to serve as the medium for the transmission of final perfect conclusions? In other words, is an imperfect man capable of perfect wisdom?

There are at least two sides to every question. Epistemology may be approached from several angles. To the inspirationalist, man is capable of at least momentary extensions of consciousness beyond the normal limitations of his organic quality. Such Paris, flights of realization are denied by the rationalist who maintains that each man's perception is limited by the quality of his perceiving part.

To the average person, it might seem that the rationalist has the better of the argument, for there is a certain reasonableness in his conclusion. But the inspirationalist is also supplied with an admirable amount of supporting testimony. He can advance numerous incidents of illumination and transcendental extension of consciousness to support his contention that, by a certain divine dispensation, some men perceive a fuller measure of the Universal Plan than is accorded to the average individual.

Nearly all of the world's greatest philosophers have been hesitant to approach the problem of ultimate knowledge. The wisest men of all time have approached wisdom with the realization of their own unworthiness. There is considerable concord among the sages in this respect. Buddha refused to discuss the nature of divinity, declaring the glory of First Cause to infinitely transcend the human capacity to understand. Confucius acted upon the same premise.

> **A PRAYER**
>
> "Teach me today, my Father, to forget the worries and wrongs of yesterday. Help me with a clearer mind and conscience to remember the duties and responsibilities of today. May thoughts of love, cheer and happiness crowd out all of the disappointments that went out of my life with the setting of yesterday's sun."

Mohammed attempted no detailed interpretation of the Universal One, Its substance, or Its activities. Socrates declared the examination of the divine attributes to be singularly unprofitable. "To define God is to defile God" summarizes the Classical approach.

As the ancients regarded Deity as identical with wisdom, and coeternal with the principle of truth, their attitude towards Epistemology can be inferred from their attitude towards God and First Cause.

While it was pretty generally accepted that the finite cannot grasp the Infinite, it did not necessarily follow that man was incapable of extending his consciousness beyond the limitations imposed by the animal existence. In the ancient Mysteries, inspiration inferred an extension of consciousness, but not necessarily a grasp of ultimates.

Thus, a man may become relatively all-knowing and yet be comparatively ignorant when estimated in terms of Absolute truth. Plato was one of the wisest men who ever lived; his intellect greatly exceeded that of the ordinary man. This does not infer, however, that Plato possessed absolute knowledge, or that his consciousness extended beyond the vista proper to man. Plato died with the books of Sophron under his head. He died studying. His quest for knowledge was identical with the impulse to live. His complete dedication to the achievement of wisdom was rewarded by a high measure of mental excellence. Yet Plato himself would have been the last to even infer his own perfection. The wisdom which he possessed probably revealed to him most of all the vastness of Truth and the incapacity of the human mind to ever comprehend it.

Epistemology opens an interesting field of operative philosophy. It explains the failure of science to accomplish the high measure of good, which knowledge and skill should accomplish. Epistemology points out that the scientist himself is the weakest element in science. The numerous delicate instruments which man has evolved as aids to human research have a small intrinsic virtue. Their value lies in the aid which they give to limited human perceptions. The scientist uses these instruments to bridge the interval between himself and the universe. With the microscope, he unites his consciousness with the infinite diversity of minutiae; with the telescope he diminishes the optical distance between himself and the star. The laboratory with its numerous delicate mechanisms, is itself an apology for the evident insufficiency of man. Sad to relate, intricate machinery cannot think. Although it can contribute a certain measure of increased vision and comprehension, it is only useful to the degree that it supports a consciousness and a rational intellect.

If the measure of what we think with is the measure of what we think, then the scientist himself is the vital factor in science. All the progress of science must be measured by the intellectual progress of the scientist.

Some of the East Indian systems of philosophy have evolved intricate theories concerning the substance of knowledge. These theories are neither truly inspirational nor rational, but belong to a curious metaphysical positivism. These premises involve: The acceptance of a supreme, unchanging, unconditional, eternal state of Truth, identical with spirit and God—all terms regarded impersonally. This Absolute knowledge though undefinable to the concrete perceptions, has at least the limitations of permanence and unchangeability. Metaphysically speaking, it is qualified by the condition of "being." Thus, is may be approached as having certain distinct boundaries. Or, men may depart from the fullness of it, thus inferring that is possesses condition.

In the Eastern systems of Absolutism, it is regarded as possible—through the annihilation of personality, individuality, and all moral, mental and physical polarity—for the human being to achieve union and identity with Absolute Truth, through special metaphysical disciplines.

While this viewpoint may seem to differ entirely from Western concepts of Epistemology, the differences are more imaginary than real. The Eastern mystic does not presume that the imperfect mind of man is capable of thinking perfect thoughts. He surmounts the difficulty by ceasing to think, and permitting Universal Wisdom to flow through him. Thus, the mind cannot know Universal Wisdom by itself, but may serve as an instrument for the perpetuation and manifestation of that which transcends itself. Thus, for example, the horse probably has no understanding of the purposes of the man who rides or drives it, but still the horse is an instrument for the achievement of the man's purposes. It cooperates even without understanding.

This is not only good Eastern metaphysics; it is excellent Christian theology. In the days of ecclesiastical glory, what Christian would have dared to presume that he understood either God or the Cardinal? Other men might question why; his duty was to do and die. Religion, it seems, has always assumed that men could be instruments in the accomplishment of divine purpose, although the substance of that purpose transcended their estimation. Thus, the prime requisite of religious wellbeing was faith, not only in the substance of things unseen, but in the truth of things unproven.

To the rationalist, faith is the acceptance of the undemonstrated or the indemonstrable. Thus, faith assumes the presence of a Divine Plan behind world affairs, remonstrating this plan by recourse to history, which undoubtedly reveals in no uncertain terms the ultimate triumph of virtue over vice and justice over injustice. The rationalist, though perfectly willing to accept history and to acknowledge the necessity of certain codes of human relationships, denies that these demonstrate any absolute wisdom at the root of life. He offers as a substitute human behaviorism, with its biological and psychological chemistries. To the rationalist, therefore, the circumstances arising from human action may be accepted not as consequences of absolute law, but merely as relative conditions arising from human characteristics.

The inspirationalist dominated ancient and medieval though, but the rationalists, realists and neorealists predominate in the modern school. There is always a question as to whether realism increases in an industrial era, or whether an industrial era increases during an age of realism. In our opinion, philosophy must precede practice, for individuals do not proceed along lines inconsistent with their preferences or beliefs.

To the Darwinian type of thinker, the mind grows up with man, and there is no intellect in the universe apart from or superior to evolving material creatures. Civilization is the socializing of the human mind. Industrialism, the industrializing of the human mind. The experiments of culture are the mind groping for reasonable courses of action, and the mind coming of age in man. This all sounds well, and the realist is rather proud of his euphony and his dictum.

The inspirationalist, conversely, following the Orphic and Platonic tradition, perceives mind as a super-essential principle which has existed in a perfect state throughout all eternity. Thus, man grows up to wisdom. Wisdom does not grow up in man. By certain courses of thought and action, the individual elevates himself to union with the various attributes of reason. Inspirationalism infers a monarchy of mind; rationalism, a democracy of impulses. The universe, to the rationalist, is governed by a parliament of opinions; mind makes the law. According to the inspirationalist, the world is governed by a hierarchy of divinely enlightened Beings make the man.

The Platonic doctrine of Ideas postulates the unfoldment of life according to certain patterns or archetypes established in the Divine Mind. According to this doctrine, the processes of evolution are molding the universe into a likeness which has existed for uncounted ages in the universal consciousness. The doctrine of Ideas may certainly be interpreted as signifying that progress is moving towards an already existent goal. True, this goal is materially intangible. But, as an end towards which all life is moving, this goal becomes worthy of the most profound consideration. Plato's theory of Archetypes would certainly justify the development of Epistemology as a practical department of philosophy. If Epistemology could only establish the prophetic import of archetypes, it would solve one of the greatest problems of human existence—namely, destiny. To the Middle Academicians, destiny was more than merely culminative. Destiny did not depend entirely upon the accident of action. Law determined the end; man, only devised the means to the accomplishment of that end. If the doctrine of Archetypes is accepted and justified, a tremendous field of speculation is opened.

Accepting a certain natural consistency throughout Universal action, it would follow that nature would contain numerous Archetypes—patterns of numerous purposes. Quite in accordance with such a doctrine, the Cosmos may be regarded as being Itself the objectification and fulfillment of a vast Archetype in which the perfect relationship and ultimate state of all beings are already clearly defined. This ultimate state and perfect relationship of all natural organisms and their consequences, might be regarded as constituting a body of absolute fact, absolute wisdom, and absolute law, beyond which no recourse is conceivable.

Most of the great Mystery Schools of the older world held opinions consistent with the Platonic idea. They taught growth by intent and not by accident. They envisioned man growing into a destiny which had been prepared for him while the worlds themselves were being formed. PROGRESS WAS A MOTION TOWARDS CONSISTENCY WITH ARCHETYPES.

Man became nobler and more illumined as the interval between himself and the pattern of his perfection grew less. To the Greeks, happiness was peace between man and his pattern. If an individual lived in a manner utterly inconsistent with the archetype of his species, that man suffered from an inharmony set up by this inconsistency. It is not what a man does that causes him to suffer—it is the inharmony between what he does and what he should do that causes suffering.

If we regard Absolute knowledge as the perfect comprehension of the pattern or Idea of being, then Epistemology determines the measure of man's ability to perceive the purpose of himself. We cannot agree with the materialist, or the behaviorist, that progress is achieved solely through the accumulation of actions and attitudes. Yet presuming that a purpose-pattern actually does exist, how can the average individual become aware of it? By what disciplines and developments can man distinguish the true reason for himself and segregate the real values of his life? If Epistemology is directly concerned with the intrinsic factors of knowledge, it must be equally concerned with the use-value of such conclusions as it may reach.

Having thus briefly summarized some elements of the philosophy of knowledge as generally considered, let us now approach the matter in a more esoteric manner. Let us try to discover what Epistemology means to the student of mystical philosophy who desires to use all the tools of wisdom in the perfection of his character.

In the initiations of the Dionysian's, man is represented as composed of a confused mixture of spiritual and material elements. The human form was molded from the blood of Bacchus and the ashes of the Titans. By the blood of Bacchus was inferred the spiritual life principle, and by the ashes of the Titans the elementary substances of the inferior or material world.

The ancients expressed this in the simple formula: form is a compound arising out of the mingling of spirit and matter. All forms must necessarily contain a certain proportion of spiritual and material agencies. It is decreed by the Universal Archetype that in the ultimate the spiritual part of each form must increase in domination over the material parts, until spirit or consciousness transmutes matter into soul, and finally absorbs even the soul itself so that only spirit remains, triumphant over the illusions of inferior nature.

Such a doctrine presupposes that the spiritual part of man is itself an aspect or fragment of the Divine Spirit and the Divine Mind. As the Divine Nature includes among its attribute's Absolute wisdom, it would follow that the divine part of man is itself all-wise and all-knowing. Socrates and his pupil Plato both accepted this tenet as the key to human salvation. Socrates did not believe that any man could be taught inasmuch as all men contain within themselves a divine wisdom which cannot be increased. Education therefore, as the word itself originally inferred, is a process by which wisdom is drawn out of man.

Every man's true teacher is his own higher Self, and when the life is brought under the control of reason, this higher Self is released from bondage to appetites and impulses, and becomes priest, sage and illuminator. Plato expressed the same idea in the words: learning is only remembering. Plotinus, the great Alexandrian Neo-Platonist, regarded the higher spiritual nature of man as a more or less complete individuality, an Over-Self. In our previous letter will be found a more complete exposition of this idea. On at least three occasions Plotinus was "lifted up to union with his God" and in those "blessed moments" the philosopher perceived a measure of truth vastly more satisfying than the small knowledge that is our common lot.

This will naturally bring up another question. If there is an absolute knowledge in the world, if there is a supreme wisdom locked within the soul of things, what is the intrinsic nature of that knowledge? Is it merely an extension or fullness of our material learning or is it a knowledge entirely apart, distinct from sciences and philosophies?

For example, does "cosmic consciousness" infer absolute knowledge of particulars or is it more a realization of the sufficiency of generals? What, in short, is the relation between Universal knowledge and the finite sciences? Would illumination result in the biologist becoming master of every secret of biology? or of the chemist becoming proficient in every mystery of chemistry? Would "cosmic consciousness" bestow technique? Would a man, lifted for a moment into the Universal Reality, be able to play any musical instrument while in that condition if he had never previously practiced upon any instrument? How should we interpret the Scriptural promise that if we seek first the kingdom of truth and righteousness, all other things shall be added unto us?

This problem is more pertinent than it may at first appear. Many people believe that if they can achieve a mystical extension of consciousness, they will become all-knowing and escape from the drudgery of effort.

Euclid told the king of Egypt that there was no royal road to learning. Does this statement contradict the Platonic doctrine of an all-wise Divine Self?

It has been my experience in meeting people interested in metaphysical subjects to find that "cosmic consciousness" is most usually interpreted as a perfection of knowledge, and that he who possesses it becomes immediately master of all worldly wisdom. Thus, we have people searching for "cosmic consciousness" to cure toothaches, lift mortgages, to overcome stuttering, or to gain proficiency in law, medicine, art, literature and music—and even the crafts. We find "cosmic consciousness" also cultivated in the hope that it will remove the sting of suffering and disappointment, so that a person who has lost everything may gain content with nothing —or perhaps the stimulus necessary to retrieve his fortunes. Although thousands of metaphysical students in all parts of the world are striving for "cosmic consciousness," as they please to call it, very few of them have read Plato sufficiently to grasp the significance of the old doctrine.

The spirit is not necessarily wise in the things of the body. It is, rather, all-wise in the things which pertain to the spirit. According to the Egyptians, men are lifted up to God through the body of Serapis, and always extensions of consciousness infer the elevation of the individual. He is lifted up to truth. But if a man be lifted up to truth, he is not at the same time going to be elevated above the sphere of matter. We cannot accept the idea of "cosmic consciousness" directing the affairs of the material man. We can acknowledge that to an individual, who has been accorded a glimpse of cosmic truth, the concerns of physical existence become comparatively unimportant.

Cosmic consciousness did not remove the hemlock cup from Socrates, but it removed the concern over death. Cosmic consciousness did not prevent Pythagoras from being burned to death with his disciples—a martyr to the highest cause of truth. But it conferred upon the great Samian sage a power to transcend all the limitations of the flesh by the magnificence of inward realization. Cosmic consciousness did not prevent Buddha from lying down by the Indian road at last to die, but it enabled this great Arhat to release his conscious soul from the Wheel of the Law. Although Plotinus was consciously united to his God, he died of the infirmities of the flesh, as do all men. Cosmic consciousness did not prevent a long and languishing illness, but it gave him the fortitude to bear all things and to face eternity with a good hope. Cosmic consciousness did not spare St. Francis of Assisi the sufferings which are the lot of mortal men. The infirmities of his frail and insufficient body gained their victory over the flesh, but the soul of the Seer had found its peace in the universal concord within and beyond.

If we acknowledge, then, that all these great, good and noble men, who accomplished the realization of the Great Plan, possessed this "cosmic consciousness" of truth, we must also acknowledge that in every case this consciousness was used entirely to enrich the inward spiritual existence and never to profit the outer life. Realization gave strength to bear, courage to endure, but never implied immunity from physical disaster.

Considering the lives and writings of numerous mystics in every civilization, past and present, it becomes evident that the inner wisdom which is possessed by the soul and is derived from the Universal Good should not be regarded as pertaining to human institutions but purely to the concerns of the inner life. The spiritual part of man is of undeterminable age. For billions of years, the spiritual germ has evolved through incalculable conditions, until at last it has emerged to its present state. Before man extends an infinite horizon; the whole spiritual existence of man must be measured in terms of the Infinite, even as the physical existence is measured in terms of the finite.

It must naturally follow that the divine consciousness of man must be directed to the vast problems of real existence. Cosmic consciousness existed long before the discovery of arts and sciences. These noble institutions which have stood in society for several thousands of years are merely passing incidents in the vast panorama of divine purpose. Whether a man lives or dies is of very little importance. Whether he masters a language, which at most will only be spoken for a few hundred years, is even less important. His community standing is nil from a cosmic standpoint. In fact, nearly everything we are interested in is unimportant except for that passing moment during which it transpires.

How irreconcilable, therefore, are the small purposes of our daily existence and the vast purposes of our spiritual being! Cosmic consciousness infers these vast purposes. In the realm of It, "you" and "I" cease. Our gains and losses are absurdities. The cosmic vista stretches out through a thousand millennia of activity. Any form of knowledge which is satisfying to our present state is convicted of insufficiency, merely because it satisfies.

This does not mean that we should not continue to improve ourselves, but it does distinctly mean that we should recognize ourselves as existing in two distinct conditions of being. The first of these conditions we shall call our present material state which is terribly important for threescore years and ten, and completely absorbs the attention of the average individual. Our second condition is an immeasurable cosmic existence, extending infinitely throughout time and space. It is very difficult to reconcile these two conditions. The greater can never be brought down to the lower; and the ascent to the greater is rendered difficult by many misunderstandings and illusions.

From the standpoint of Epistemology, we must therefore distinguish between knowledge in its Universal and particular aspects. Universal knowledge is the realization of cosmic identity. It is man's knowledge of the at-one-ment of himself and life. It is real knowledge, transcending statistics and classified data. This universal knowledge is release through the heart, as supreme conviction, under certain circumstances which are called "mystical experiences."

The second form of knowledge is particular and is limited to the matters of this life. It is conditioned and circumscribed. The achievement of it is an arduous experiment in remembering. There can be no absolute physical knowledge because all physical conditions are relative and impermanent; all material things change and are conditioned by circumstance.

The material man, devoted to the quest for knowledge, grasps at the fleeting form of fact, seeking to hold some exactness upon which he can found dogma and doctrine. But facts are ever illusive. The great spiritual facts of life which belong to the sphere of Absolute truth are meaningless and useless to a mind and consciousness unprepared to receive them.

Thus, from our small and inadequate point of view, we accept material superstitions as truths and ardently defend our own attitudes. At the same time, we reject as superstitions the cosmic truths of life and call men visionary and impractical who seek the inner mysteries of existence.

Yours sincerely,
Manly P. Hall

SOME PHILOSOPHICAL FRAGMENTS

Dangers of New Thought – Metaphysical and Psychology
THE FIRST PRINCIPLES OF SUPERSCIENCE - I

THERE are in nature certain forces capable of molding human consciousness into the directions outlined by one who is capable of becoming master of said forces. There are certain methods outlined by the gods themselves, by following which man may learn to govern the expressions of these subtle and invisible forces of the superphysical worlds and make them active in modern world affairs. A person capable of manifesting these energies and making them work for him to any prescribed extent is called a Magician, or more correctly a Magus, or a juggler of natural law. A person who passes through the school outlined by the powers that be, and who gradually comes into these powers is called first an adept, and later an Initiate, who takes his place among those who dedicate their newly acquired powers to the service of humanity.

The Masters work slowly but those who finally acquire after, not weeks but years and ages, of conscientious application and purification, these great forces, can be trusted with them and seldom fail to make the proper use of them. There is only one way of preventing the misuse of power which is the great danger that confronts one who has recently come into a position of authority, and that is, that with the coming of the power itself there must be also born in man a realization of responsibility, and an understanding of nature's plan equal to the power that is his, so that consciously and willingly the soul will dedicate that force to the service of good. Power brings egotism to the young and responsibility to the old. Nearly all who spend a few years in modern Metaphysics come out broken in mind and body, self-centered egotists, who do not know where they are mentally, have lost all desire to work and wander from one teacher to another searching for knowledge until at last the insane asylum or the state grave-yard claims them. They no longer have the power of thinking for themselves and follow like little puppies everyone who has a peculiar opinion.

The First Great Danger—Opinions

Opinions are not facts. But the majority of Metaphysicians express them as such and there is no earthly need for such an attitude. All are students together, the teacher and the follower, and when the instructor dogmatically states that this is so, and that is not so, or the Bible meant this, and not that, he speaks with authority on a subject about which he has no information save an opinion, which to him may be reasonable but not to anyone else. The great wisdom of the world is not in the hands of super-opinionated persons. Nor does it come by hunches. It has its representatives in the world but they are not gushy persons or rattlebrains but silent dignified teachers whose message is true because they have lived every line of its rules themselves.

The ancient wisdom does not need to be proven; it proves itself upon application. But the endless contradictions which confront the students of metaphysics can never be proven or accepted by thinking individuals. If metaphysics would admit that it is an open forum for opinions and nothing else the public would be protected, but each of the scores of contradicting philosophers that compose it claim to have the truth, the whole truth and nothing but the truth, proving this claim by trying to teach their own ideas to others who are sincerely seeding, not for ideas, but the base rock of common sense upon which to build a permanent structure. Looking over a series of advertisements put out by teachers along this line during the last few years, l am going to correct, some of them for you. The first one says:

"Let me show you how to be a success." It sounds good, but an analysis of the party of the first part will show that the individual did not know himself but had some ideas on the subject. If his ad had been honestly written, is would have read something like this: "I have some ideas about success. I do not know whether they will help you or not, but you have my permission to come and hear me talk about them!"

Another one reads something like this: "The Fourth Dimension Found" by John Doe. "Come and hear this remarkable speaker, etc." Here again, fancy is passed off for fact. John hasn't the slightest idea what the fourth dimension is, but he claims to have had a vision, the source of authenticity of which he knows nothing. His advertisement should read like this: "I believe that I know what the fourth dimension is. Come and hear me express my OPINION ON THAT INTERESTING SUBJECT. "

Two crimes are committed by these thoughtless persons who would be useful servants of the Masters if they were not so self-centered. The first is, that they slander the reality and daily disgrace the spiritual truths that they claim to serve. The second is, they prevent the human soul from attaining the truth by leading him astray into the avenues of personal opinions which they are pawning off as facts.

Day after day individuals and organizations come to me, trying to impress me with the value of their ideas and the divine inspirations behind their cults. They express themselves fluently on subjects they know nothing about and then wonder how it is my soul is so clouded that I cannot see the divine wisdom of their soul or the magnificence of their opinion. Their whole scheme is an idea or maybe their interpretation of someone else's idea. They finally decide that I am wrong. Maybe I am, but out of the hundreds of opposing doctrines it is rather delightful to find a Wrong one. None of them will admit that they are in error—that is to the public—but if the public were mind readers, they might discover something.

WHEN THE TEACHERS DISAGREE, WHAT SHALL THE pupils do? If someone would find an answer to this question, the Metaphysical problem would be solved, and several other occult problems with it. Joseph's coat of many colors must have had something to do with New Thought. But what is the poor student to do when each teacher that comes along is inspired by the same God, or at least claims so, each teaching a different message, each claiming theirs to be better than any of the others, no two agreeing even on fundamentals and each claiming to teach the truth. When he does make a choice, he has nothing to guide him but speculation and some inducement of the most questionable spiritual nature. Is there any wonder that mere men's heads go round and round and that they finally go insane while trying to unravel the mystic maze that claims to lead to heaven but is much more often a blind alley leading into someone's pocket.

The world is filled with these wanderers, who do not know which way to turn. They have taken the only possible course; they have cut away from all these dissenting factions and are stumbling along as best they can. Their lives have been absolutely ruined and they are far worse off than they were in the days when they were still in the orthodox churches. They wander around like lost souls waiting for a God who never existed, save in someone's opinion, to care for them and protect them. And society as a mass must play the part of a God of another man's mind and care for these poor souls who have been robbed of their earthly possessions and individual minds.

(To be continued)

LONDON, MARCH 1, 1935

Dear Friend,

Esthetics is the sixth department of philosophy and may be defined as that branch of learning which is devoted to an examination of the substance of the beautiful and the effect of beauty upon the spiritual, intellectual and moral life of man. Under the general term, esthetics are included the several arts devoted to the theory and practice of beauty cultivated by the ancients.

Beauty is the most civilizing force in nature. The theory of esthetics leads to the appreciation of beauty; the practice of esthetics leads to the interpretation of beauty. Under the theory of esthetics, therefore, are considered standards of symmetry and proportion, relations of value and form, and the harmonies of quality, sound, color, and such other media as are appropriate to the interpretation of beauty. Under the practice of esthetics are considered the several disciplines of interpretation by which beauty is released through skill, or, as it is more commonly termed, technique.

The departments of esthetic expression are generally termed the arts. Art differs from science in that art arises from the impulses of the soul and science from the reasonings of the intellect. We may say that to do a thing skillfully is science, and when science and art contribute equally to the accomplishment of any desired end. Art adorns science and glorifies religion. Art perfects nature. A great artist is a high priest in the temple of the universe.

In ancient times, esthetics included the art of music, vocal and instrumental; the art of drama, sacred and profane; the art of sculpture, architectural and impressionistic; the art of painting, drawing and coloring; the art of the dance, artistic and gymnastic; the art of decoration, including adornment, design, et cetera; the art of oratory, from which later evolved poetry and literature; and lastly, the sacred arts, including all the esthetics of veneration. Together, these constituted one supreme art—the art of living.

In Egypt, the priests evolved what is termed the Hermetic art which descended to medieval Europe as alchemy. According to Arthur Dee, the Great Work of the Hermetic philosophers was to perfect nature through art. It is the refining influence of beauty and idealism that is gradually transforming animal man into a divine being.

> "My son, some Kings are commonplace, and not all laborers are worthy of their hire. But this I say to you; that if you are in league with gods to learn life and to live it, neither kings nor commoners can possibly prevent you, though they try their utmost. You shall find help unexpectedly, from strangers who, it may be know not why."—Tsiang Samdup.

Esthetics is the mysterious tincture of the alchemistical philosophers by which the base elements of life are transmuted into the gold of truth and beauty. Esthetics is also the Universal Medicine, for only beauty and nobility can bring health to the human soul, which is sickened with the evils of the world.

An individual or community which does not appreciate and practice beauty cannot long survive. The whole philosophy of esthetics can be summed up in the simple statement attributed to the great prophet of Islam, Mohammed:

"If I had two coats, I would sell one of them and buy white hyacinths for my soul."

Civilization complicates all issues, and under the intensiveness of our modern culture even the simplest values become involved in a confusion of opinions. We have lost the power to enjoy beauty. The arts have become confused and, for the most part discordant. They no longer minister to our common need; rather, they torment us with their complexities and discomfort our souls with their asymmetries. When false standards are set up, the intrinsic fineness of things is sacrificed. Generally speaking, modern esthetics is corrupt. Artists are failing art, and for that reason, art is failing man.

The first principle of art is beauty. It must be beautiful to be art. Technique and skill can exist apart from art, but technique and skill are not art in themselves. They are merely the means by which art is released into tangible expression. The beginning and end of art is always beauty. What, then, is beauty? The noblest speculations on this subject are contained in the celebrated treatise of Plotinus on the beautiful. From this great Neo-Platonist we learn that beauty is essentially perfect order—in things and of things. Beauty is a certain virtue present in all bodies, in all forms, and in all substances. Beauty is the true being which animates all living creatures. It is the dynamic pattern, the esthetic framework by which the world is supported. Beauty is that peculiar fitness by which perfected natures are distinguished from imperfect natures, and perfect forms from imperfect forms. According to Plotinus, there is a certain divine consistency which is more evident in some structures than in other structures. Beginnings move naturally towards certain ends; forces unfold through forms; wisdom blossoms in space; the Divine Will, projecting itself into matter, becomes a symmetrical geometric pattern in which all the elements of beauty are perfectly present.

The human mind, itself composed of the Divine Nature, and imbued at least subjectively with the principle of esthetics, accepts the proportions of nature as a certain artistic canon, thinking and estimating in terms of this canon. The intellect carries what may be termed a certain expectancy towards proportion, rhythm, and normalcy. The intellect, therefore, experiences a definite disappointment if the expectancy is not fulfilled. We interpret this disappointment as displeasure or esthetic offense. If, on the other hand, the expectancy is fulfilled there is a satisfaction which we interpret as pleasure.

For example, a gently curving line presumes the continuance of that curve or its development into some logical form. If a sudden angle is interposed there is a definite shock to the esthetic sensibilities. A broken arch is a disappointment. It is true that a broken line is more powerful than a continuous one, because of the blow which it administers to the subjective awareness. But strength is not always beauty. The purpose of art is not merely to attract attention or to force comment. The true purpose of art is to satisfy soul hunger. So, the broken arch does not express the highest form of art and is not truly beautiful.

As another example, the mental expectancy of man may be focused upon a massive column, finely proportioned, and giving the definite impression that it is intended to support a great weight. If this pillar is caused to support some small and inconsequential structure, the esthetic consciousness is again offended. Everything must have a purpose, and a column which has no purpose sufficient to justify its existence is not truly beautiful. As Socrates has so wisely observed, a thing must be necessary to be beautiful. Nature has devised nothing which does not serve some purpose. This is the highest form of art. The universe, which is a perfect example of utility, is also the most beautiful of all structures cognizable by man. In esthetics, that which is impossible, improbable, or deformed offends. And in character, that which is ignoble offends. That which offends cannot be beautiful. The grotesque may teach a lesson, but it cannot serve as a direct inspiration to consciousness.

This brings up another question. Why is man offended by that which is not beautiful? According to Socrates, there exists within every human being a divine nature composed of the three qualities of unity, beauty, and utility. The human soul, according to this old sage, is a perfectly symmetrical divine body containing within itself every element of beauty. Thus, every man, regardless of the depravity of his outer life or the immaturity of his esthetic appreciation, possesses to some measure what may be termed an instinct towards the appreciation of beauty. That which is unbeautiful offends the soul because it offends the truth which abides in the soul. This offense against the symmetry of the inner Self causes the reaction of displeasure which is felt when in the presence of an asymmetrical structure.

We may then ask—is there an absolute standard of beauty? Is the human soul capable of recognizing ultimate perfection in the esthetic arts, or does man's sense of beauty grow up with his experience and evolution? If we examine the arts of the various nations, ancient and modern, we must acknowledge that esthetics is subject to the law of evolution. The human being is growing up to the appreciation of beauty even as he is evolving to a fuller comprehension of all abstract values. Genius has existed in every age and each civilization has produced a few exceptional individuals who have possessed a high measure of esthetic vision. As time goes on an ever-greater percentage of persons will sense the subtle values which dignify life. The arts will finally flourish and in the Golden Age, which men have dreamed of since the beginning, we shall dwell together not only in peace but in a world made beautiful.

To the philosopher, Divinity itself is the absolute standard of all perfection. One philosopher said, "Only God is good." And in another age, another philosopher said, "Only God is beautiful." By the term God we must understand the all-knowing, all animating Spirit of the world by whose wisdom universal law is maintained. The beauties of nature and of man, therefore, are really the beauty of God in nature and God in man. The word God means good and good infers perfection into all the virtues. To the ancient's virtue inferred obedience. "The beginning of wisdom is to revere the gods through obedience," declared the Platonic doctrine. To be good, therefore, is not a platitudinous injunction. It means to fulfill the law, and to fulfill the law means, according to the Socratic philosophers, to do that which is necessary and beautiful.

Esthetics graces action by overcoming all excess and intemperance. Esthetics is the living of the principle of beauty and results in living beautifully. For this reason, living is called an art. Scientists would have us believe that living is a science, and commercialists believe that living is a trade. But to the degree that men live well, they live according to esthetic standards. Esthetics as action is moderation—the Golden Mean, the temperate zone of the wise. Esthetics as morality is virtue—victory over inordinate emotions and desires. Esthetics as thought is wisdom, by which all exaggerations of attitudes are brought to a common order. Esthetics as form is symmetry, in which there is no disproportion of parts. Esthetics as civilization is concord and the dwelling together in cooperation and peace. Esthetics is rhythm, harmony and melody. In every course of action, it is that desirable and happy state in which, there is no discord or inconsistency.

Through the esthetic impulse in the human soul, man is impelled to the perfection of the arts. He seeks to beautify his body, his home, his community, and his world. But art involves not only appreciation but also discipline. Discipline is the development of the skill to interpret, and also, the development of the value-sense, the power to discriminate. In music, discipline is the training of the voice or the hand and the ear. Sculpture, the faculties of form and perception must be developed, and a certain technique of procedure mastered. Drama and the dance demand the disciplining of the emotional faculties and perfect control of the physical body, also to some degree adornment. Appropriate disciplines are also necessary in the sacred arts and oratory.

It should be remembered, however, that discipline does not confer art; it merely supports and rationalizes artistic impulse. Discipline comes to nothing, and all training is ineffectual, unless technique is vitalized by soul power. Esthetics is a universal principle which men can partake of in varying degrees, according to their development. Artists are not made by discipline, but genius can go to seed for lack of order and technical direction.

We must try to understand the evolution of esthetic appreciation, for without appreciation there can be no interpretation and art is interpretation. Two forces are constantly at work in the molding of human character. The early Church called these two forces good and evil, or God and the devil. Philosophy, which impersonalizes all universal principles, interprets these contending forces as inner impulse and outer circumstance. There is a constant conflict between man and his world, between the individual and the mass.

The two irreconcilable opposites in civilization today are truth and the majority.

This brings us to one of the major issues of esthetic philosophy: idealism versus realism. The idealist affirms that all things are essentially good and that a divine wisdom, essentially beautiful in its workings, is present throughout nature. All life is moving towards unity, beauty, and virtue. The realist, on the other hand, maintains that nothing is really any better than it seems to be. Realism as a doctrine is the most disillusioning of all codes. Realism is established upon the testimony of unrefined sense perceptions, while idealism is established upon a sympathetic and enlightened recognition of the true values which lie beneath appearances.

What then, asks the modern artist, is the highest expression of art? Is it the effort to depict a beauty which is often not apparent or the attempt to copy asymmetry which is usually painfully evident? This argument brings up still another issue. When considering esthetics as art, how shall we define an artist? Is he a creator or a copyist? Is he a depicter or an interpreter? Is he an educator or merely a technician? Should he portray what he sees or what he feels? If he portrays what he sees, with what kind of eyes does he see? If he portrays what he feels, with what kind of a soul does he feel? Is art merely design, a distribution of masses, or a clever combination of light and shadow? These questions are seldom satisfactorily answered in the schools of modern art.

There is a great division in modern opinion as to whether or not art should serve as a medium for the communication of ideas. In other words, should painting, sculpture, music or the dance tell a story or does its excellence depend upon its meaninglessness? The modern tendency in art is to depart from all preachment and interpretation. To the average critic, a picture is worthless if it tells a story. To the true esthetician, modern art is therefore, for the most part unsatisfying because it contributes nothing to the intellectual or spiritual values of life. In a recent exhibition, a place of honor was awarded to a painting which represented a side of beef hanging in a butcher's window. A small canvas of a badly drawn orange on a cracked plate was also regarded as exceptional. Fried eggs are also regarded as an enchanting form of still life, while paintings resembling Spanish omelets are labeled as creative realizations of sunsets.

Such productions not only lack interest, they actually lack technical merit. The creators of these so-called pictures have never mastered the technique of draughtsmanship, and for the most part have no fundamental knowledge of color. Even these shortcomings might be forgiven, however, if the artist really possessed an idea. There is something glorious in even an imperfect effort to do something that is noble and beautiful. We are all imperfectly striving towards noble and beautiful ends. The greatest shortcoming of the average modern artist is lack of an idea. They break the ancient Chinese axiom that nothing should be done without an adequate reason.

There is good modern art, but it is comparatively rare due to the present superficial attitudes which dominate racial culture. All modern artists, to the contrary notwithstanding, there is no satisfying art which does not tell a story, create a beautiful mood, or reveal a high inspirational quality in the soul of the artist.

Esthetics as theory, infers a creative impulse supported by technical knowledge. Of course, only a few highly evolved mortals possess the soul power to achieve greatly in the arts. Nevertheless, beauty is necessary to every human being. If we cannot perform, we must at least appreciate. No one can be truly normal unless he has some esthetic appreciation. The love of the beautiful and the expression of beauty through some art enriches the life and protects the spiritual values of man from the corroding influences of this present commercial era.

It seems in order at this point to make a few practical suggestions concerning the application of esthetic principles to the life of the average individual. Every serious student of the spiritual sciences should realize the full import of beauty as a ministering force in life. The ancient Egyptians cultivated esthetics in all of its branches as part of the state religion. The Greeks passed laws prohibiting the construction of asymmetrical buildings or the exhibition or performance of art, drama or music which did not conform to certain esthetic standards. The Greeks punished with exile and disgrace anyone who willfully perverted any standard of beauty. The Spartans destroyed at birth all deformed infants lest deformity exhibited to the populace in their later years should corrupt the state. These various measures were dictated by a profound understanding and contributed largely to the excellence of these empires and states. We all admire the nobility and beauty which distinguished the classical systems of philosophy and religion. If we would share the wisdom of the ancients, we must rise to their esthetic standards.

The absence of art or esthetic consciousness in the average home is a greater tragedy than may at first appear. This general indifference to beauty is an important factor in the widespread decadence of culture and integrity throughout the so-called civilized world. People who are content to live in a home filled with gaudy cheapness and evidences of bad taste will find that their personal standards of life and thought are infected and corrupted by this unfitting and unlovely atmosphere. Every student of philosophy and mysticism should realize the necessity of including beauty in his budget. He should realize that art is a living force and should place it above material luxury.

As a homely but literal illustration of this point, study the average home. The rooms are filled with cheap chromos in over-gilded frames, and inexpensive trifles accumulated at holidays and bridge parties. Ten dollars would be a high price for the total collection. Few fine books ever invade the premises. Cheap editions, if any, badly printed and in gaudy covers, fill the library "shelf." Practically no good sculpture ever reaches the private home in America.

Is this condition really necessary in a country which, even during the present depression, has the highest per capita wealth of any country in the world? The excuse is that, by the time the rent is paid, the installments on the Frigidaire, radio, automobile, furniture, et cetera are met, and the pressing bills of the month taken care of, there are no funds left with which to indulge an esthetic urge. The truth, however, is that there is no urge. If a true urge existed, it would take precedence over creature comforts, conveniences and luxuries.

While it is undoubtedly true that many people cannot afford anything beyond the bare necessities of life, there are a great number who can afford good cars, good clothes, entertainment, a radio, and various social expenditures. All these can afford beauty. We should cease to think of art as a luxury of the rich and realize that it is also a necessity of the poor. The strength of the nation is its middle class, and it is this great middle class that needs the refining, purifying influence of fine art. Beauty is a constant inspiration and an ever-present help in time of trouble.

Any person who can afford the creature comforts such as are common in the average American home can afford, by careful planning, to possess at least one fine and beautiful example of esthetic art to inspire him and to become a part of his life. If the man who has been buying a new car each year will forego this luxury for a season and buy a good painting, a fine piece of sculpture, a rare book, or some object of beauty which pleases him, he will discover that the satisfying of the esthetic sense is one of the most practical ways of spending money. Possibly one of the reasons why so few people are satisfied to stay at home is because there is so little of beauty in the home to sanctify and refine the environment.

A house that is filled with numerous bric-a-brac and maudlin sentimentalities needs a thorough going-over. The ancient Mayan ceremony should be performed, which consisted of burning all personal effects at certain intervals. It is a common fault to believe that a room must be littered with a thousand eyesores in order to be furnished. The wise man never forgets the dignity of space. Blank walls are much more artistic than the things which usually cover them. In a simple, uncluttered environment, one fine art object will stand out—its beauty a benediction upon the whole environment. The Oriental art connoisseur, whose taste bears witness to thousands of years of civilizing culture, seldom permits himself the luxury of more than one fine painting or beautiful ceramic to even a large room, and all of his furnishings will be consistent one with the other. He will never mix his schools of art or his periods of furnishings. To do so is to irritate the soul.

It is also painfully evident that the average person makes absolutely no effort to cultivate any of the arts in himself. The radio takes the place of music in the home. Few people are willing to train themselves in vocal or instrumental performance, or in the dance. The excuse given is that there is no financial future for such talents. No thought is given to the really important issue—the development of the esthetic nature and the personal satisfaction and improvement to be derived from the ability to perform.

The average individual does not make a constructive use of his emotional energies. The proper application of esthetic laws and principles will transmute instinct and appetite into creative impulse and artistic expression. Nearly all of the evils of human disposition arise from the repression or misapplication of emotional energy. The hates, fears, griefs and worries of mankind bear witness to undirected and untransmuted emotional energy. The disciplines of esthetics give legitimate expression to the impulsiveness of human nature. We cannot be truly dedicated to beauty and at the same time fail to develop a certain inward grace. The esthetic arts are the normal and natural channels for the manifestation of man's complicated emotional reflexes.

Nearly all human beings are in some way emotionally inhibited. These inhibitions often break out in unbeautiful action and thought. These periodic outbursts, usually attended by unfortunate consequences, can be prevented if the emotional life is allowed a beautiful and creative expression through someone of the several esthetic arts. These arts can fill empty lives and the empty places in otherwise full lives. There are people who feel that they are alone and neglected, and view the whole existence as a more or less tragic span. These persons can enrich themselves spiritually and emotionally through the theory and practice of artistic expression.

Very truly yours,

Manly P. Hall

SOME PHILOSOPHICAL FRAGMENTS
Dangers of New Thought – Metaphysical and Psychology
THE FIRST PRINCIPLES OF SUPERSCIENCE - II
(Continued from Feb. Letter Supplement)

This is not written in the spirit of criticism, but is a plain expression of facts as they are. Every day they come to us groping in spirit and body, floating like broken hulks on the sea of life. We are sorry for them and ask that those who are truly trying to help will join with us to help these people back, to their feet again, not filling their heads with more opinions but standing them upon their feet and aiding them to think for themselves again. When man loses his conceit and becomes human again, he will realize that because he is able to think is no proof that he is able to think well.

WHERE OUR MODERN TEACHERS COME FROM. Our modern celebrities can be generally divided into two groups when we commit crime to the problem of source. One group are inspired. In the majority, experience proves that their inspiration was a personal opinion strengthened by encouragement and conceit on the part of the individual himself. The other group is those who have taken lessons themselves from some other teacher. In the majority of cases, this just proves to be the passing of opinions and acceptance of these opinions as facts by the student. How many of you would want to be operated on by a man who had only studied surgery for two weeks, and that only from someone who claimed to know. Yet we will trust our souls to one who claimed to have a vision, or who goes into trances.

Many metaphysicians are sincerely trying to help, but the ground is so fertile that there has been a great influx of spiritual carpet-baggers and metaphysical patent medicine venders who are in for all they can get out of it. One of them told me that there was a fool born every minute and if he did not get it, someone else would. The "it" of course referring to the contents of your pocket book THE MASS OF OCCULT STUDENTS TODAY ARE NOT ON THE path. They think they are, but it is again only someone's opinion. Even those who are looked up to as most advanced, and "old souls' are advancing into blind alleys. Either the students did not get what the teacher said or else they did and the teacher said nothing. It is of course, an open problem as to which that is. The worst part is that they go out of life with less than they came in with, for they came in with an opportunity and wasted that.

THE SECOND GREAT DANGER—PSYCHOLOGY

The greatest danger of psychology is that it is true. The mind of man, groping in the darkness of limitation, found the touchstone, or at least some did, that the gods had concealed since the days of Atlantis. A science whereby man may demand of the Infinite, and the Infinite must obey, has been founded upon that discovery. But the new blessing that man grasped at was a deadly thing, bearing UPON IT A CURSE, THE CURSE OF THE GODS. These powers belong to the gods and they bestow them upon those who are found worthy. But when man steals them from the Infinite, their new found power destroys them. Only the God man prepared after the manner of the law is fitted to grasp in his fingers those subtle forces that are now in the hands of fools. Instead, then of a blessing to help us on our way, it only gives us another and more terrible way of expressing the beast within our own souls.

For ages, the beast has been bound to earth by his own limitations and ignorance, but now he rises armed with the powers of the gods.

HEAVEN ALONE KNOWS WHAT THE END WILL BE. This mighty power, that our forefathers never dreamed of, sank Atlantis, has destroyed all the races that have so far peopled the earth, and now like a plague it is descended upon our race to confront it with the great temptation. It is the demon at the shoulder of the master; it is the power of God himself, and how does selfish man know how to wield it. Crimes that once he hung for can now be done silently and unsuspected, things that he once labored for as an honest man he now seeks to secure through his subtle force; he strikes where those who do not know cannot retaliate. To the egotism and brutality of the beast is added now the scepter of a demi-god. But of course, in time, things will right themselves and the plan to go on. But if the present attitude is continued, the race will dissolve itself in the swirl of occult, called by those who cannot manage them, and left like plagues upon nature's face.

The modern teachers of Psychology are unconsciously damning the race by teaching man to use the forces but not teaching how to use them wisely. They have but one legitimate use, but no one would bother them if that use was explained and the present application made impossible. These forces are to be used only as directed by the masters for the unfoldment of man himself and the development of the earth. How many of the students of Psychology are using them that way? Not enough to discuss. ALL PERSONAL USES OF SUPERPHYSICAL OR MENTAL POWER FOR THE ATTAINMENT OF PERSONAL ENDS is criminal. And all who make use of it in such ways secure with it the curse of the gods. The curse is this, that they will destroy themselves with their attempts to satisfy their own egotism. The curse is sure; they have already hypnotized themselves with the powers they sought to exert over others, and while millions will suffer with them, they will suffer most of all. The answer There is but one solution to the problem and it has nothing to do with creeds or clans. It is too late to conceal the knowledge- It is already on the lips of children. MAN MUST BE TAUGHT TO ACCEPT WITH THIS DIVINE POWER THE RESPONSIBILITY OF THE GODS. It is only in this way that he can prevent his own destruction. If he will only mold his life into the pattern of the Masters, he may yet learn to wield this awful force as they do, that it brings forth good and not evil, a feast and not a famine. But will man think? Will he sacrifice himself now in order to save himself later? We hope, but we are sorely afraid that he will not bend to the will of the Masters until he has destroyed all. Man does not know how to use these finer forces; he is playing with destruction but will allow naught to guide him or direct him. He wants what he wants and turns all the powers that he has to the attainment of his own desires. The things he wants will kill him, for they are all of the earth, earthy. He listens to none but, happy with the new found toy which he believes will make him happy, he shakes off the hand of prudence and dashes blindly over the cliff to his death.

What good does it do to warn, they only laugh. What if the handwriting is upon the wall, they will not heed until the walls begin to fall. And then they turn and pray for mercy, those who would not listen to the guidance of understanding. So, Psychology will every day become more popular, teaching man to gain what he wants, but failing to teach him that only God knows what he truly needs. If he gains what he wants, it will kill him and he never seeks for what he needs. So, the curse of the gods is upon him for stealing their power and not accepting their understanding.

END

INTERESTING NEWS ITEMS

In one of my earlier letters, I called attention to my purchase of a Cabbalistic manuscript by the Comte de St.-Germain. This manuscript was from the library of Mr. Lionel Hauser, which was sold at Sotheby's in London by auction last April. While in Paris I visited Mr. Hauser and discussed with him the origin of this manuscript and several others of his important papers. Mr. Hauser is the owner of an important Masonic register containing the minutes and notes of important Masonic meetings in Paris between 1715 and 1789. The Marquis de la Fayette was received into this Lodge on June 24, 1782, and among the important signatures contained in the register is the signature of Comte de St. Germain. The date of the entry is several years later than the supposed date of the mysterious count's death. Mr. Hauser also possesses a curious Masonic token or pass-coin bearing St. Germain's name and used by the members of his Lodge for purposes of identification. The coin is silver, about the size of a quarter dollar, and is ornamented with Masonic emblems.

* * *

We are having a complete photostatic copy made of what is probably the most important Hermetic manuscript in the Bibliothèque National. This is the celebrated Book of Abraham the Jew, magnificently illustrated with water-color miniatures on vellum, exhibiting the innermost secrets of the Hermetic art. We hope to translate and publish this work, which up to the present time has existed only in a few inaccessible manuscripts.

NEW YORK, APRIL 1, 1935

Dear Friend,

The seventh and last branch of philosophy we have decided to term Theurgy, or Wisdom, as Divine Magic. The word Theurgy is of most honorable antiquity and was gradually narrowed from a general sense until, by the Neo-Platonists and Gnostics, it came to have the meaning which we now infer. Theurgy is the "blessed magic" of the Hermetic Egyptians. In our ladder of philosophy, it is the seventh and highest of the rungs that men must climb if they would reach up to truth.

In the old systems of wisdom, intellectual energy manifested through seven philosophical "truths" or, more correctly, six extensions and one central principle from which all the others derive their authority. This is explained in the Sepher Yetzirah in the description of the eternal temple of the ever-living truth. The "directions" are explained in the following manner: There is North, East, South and West, above and below, and in the midst of the Immovable Tabernacle of the Ageless One. The first six departments of philosophy correspond to the directions or dimensions of wisdom, and Theurgy, the consummating part, is the immovable tabernacle, the very axis of rotating intellect.

Thus, Theurgy, or its equivalent, is to be found as the very heart of every great philosophical or mystical system. To the Rosicrucian initiates, Theurgy was the "Silentium Post Clamores" of Michael Maier—the silence which follows after sound—peace after confusion—achievement after effort. To Plato, Theurgy was the Unmoved Mover of intellect. To the Oriental mystic, it is samadhi or Nirvana which consummates the restlessness of questing. Wherever men have sought for truth, they have come to realize that the search ends in a transcendent condition of achievement in suspension, the accomplishment of power which continues as power but ceases to be the cause of lower activity.

Philosophy is a universe in itself. As there is a physical world extending about us in nature, and as nature, so there is an intellectual world extending about us in thought and as thought. As mastery of the physical world brings with it a temporal superiority, so the mastery of the mental world brings with it a certain intellectual superiority. As physical society consists of numerous strata of diversified merit and unmerited, so the intellectual world has its races, its classes, its castes and its types.

> Men think they work for money or some other momentary need; but they deceive themselves, it being curious to witness how unanimously human beings substitute the shadow for the truth—which truth is, that no other impulse governs us than the necessity of growth. Remember it is not the thing done, but the doing that the gods weigh, and that many have failed to reach their goal who none the less accomplished more than he who, coming to a journey's end, thought that the mere end should justify him. -Tsiang Samdup.

As surely as men strive physically for that peace and security which has been the Utopian vision for countless ages, so, in the world of thought, men struggle for intellectual security. Security is sufficiency, and that which is insufficient or, inadequate, or inconsistent can never enjoy security.

The branches of philosophy are like continents, races, or species in physical nature. They are intellectual environments through which man must evolve mentally as upon earth he evolves physically. As the world is made up of all its races and nations, so the empire of wisdom is made up of all the branches of thinking and knowing. This is the true key to the various obscure references to the "wise mans world" scattered through the writings of initiates and adepts. To the layman whose consciousness is bound closely to the objects of external sense perception, the physical world with its problems seems very real and the world of wisdom remote and indefinite. But as man lives more and more in mind and less and less in matter, the intellectual universe emerges as a magnificent empire and physical concerns in their turn become remote and indefinite.

Wisdom not only brings the human mind gradually up to truth. It also reveals the laws which govern truth, for truth is perfect motion in the universe. By motion we infer what the wise intended by that word—not a running to and fro in confusion but rather a transcendent vibration, a motion within movement, a motion without movement, an indescribable pulsing which supports being.

Through the six directions or branches of philosophy is approached the radiant center of wisdom, therefore these branches correspond to the six conditions of being depicted by the Vhava Chakra of Tibetan Lamaism. According to this system, there are six states of being, and Buddhahood which transcends them all. He who masters the seventh possesses a true knowledge of the other six. But no mind limited by any of the other six can possess a knowledge of the seventh.

It is therefore known to the wise that there is no final satisfaction even in the possession of knowledge, for knowledge is accumulated from the six paths which lead to truth. Thus, a man who possesses an accumulation of so-called fact is not necessarily happy. Rather, knowledge depresses the average person unless that knowledge is tinctured and transmuted by a certain understanding and true illumination is achieved. This may be described in terms of alchemy. Within the curious symbolic bottles and vessels of the Hermetic philosophers, seven radiations or refinements of base elements must take place before the Wise Man's Stone, or the Ruby Medicine is achieved. The seventh condition of the Medicine or Stone is described as absolutely transcendent. The elements have been transmuted into a pure spiritual substance which contains all power and property within itself. This sublime essence is merely a symbolic term to signify pure consciousness, which possesses the perfect power of transmutation and is the all-sufficient Medicine of the Paracelsian adepts.

In philosophy Theurgy is this Medicine. It is the pure spiritual gold extracted from the baser compounds of arts and sciences. It is absolute wisdom which, like a Hermetic medicine, cures the diseases of the mind, its doubts and inconsistencies. All knowledge, therefore, avails not unless it be quickened and rendered alive and perfect by those ageless mysteries by which, as the Greeks have expressed it, men are lifted upward "through the body of the blessed God" (Nature), and are finally mingled with that Divine Consciousness which sustains the world upon the eternal foundations of wisdom alone.

Throughout this series of letters, it has been my special purpose to emphasize the Pythagorean viewpoint that philosophy is not only the science of thinking but the science of perfect living. Man's physical body is a chemical compound and the subtler elements of this compound are profoundly affected by thoughts, attitudes, emotions, impulses and actions. Philosophy as a rate of vibration must be set up in the body and in the soul as well as in the mind.

We seldom associate thought and metabolism, nor do we realize that body and spirit are bound together by certain inseparable sympathies. As Fludd, the Rosicrucian, has shown in his curious diagrams, form is externalized consciousness, and consciousness is an internalized form. Consciousness circulates through its seven bodies as a man might wander through the seven rooms of his house. Although the body is the least of the seven apartments, which the poet has termed the "mansions of the soul," it is nevertheless an integral part of man's complete economy. Philosophy flowing into the body brings to the lower man a sense of physical fitness, even as when flowing into the mind it produces, the condition of mental sufficiency.

Theurgy is philosophy as that ever-flowing fountain of wisdom, which, springing up from the deep sources of the soul, waters and renders fertile all parts of the nature. Thus, philosophy is that "ever flowing good" of the Chaldean Oracles—the fountain of everlasting life referred to in the Gospels. Those who drink of it shall thirst no more.

The term thirst should be interpreted to signify the quest for truth which only wisdom can satisfy. The Theurgist, therefore, is one who is satisfied with wisdom, whose quest has ended in achievement, and whose whole being is radiant with a perfected wisdom.

We may well say that knowledge is gathered from contact with external sources of information, but that true wisdom comes only from within. Dr. Rowley, chaplain to Lord Bacon, in describing the profundity of his Lordship's wisdom, explained that his knowledge came not from books, though he read much, but rather from some hidden source deep within himself. Wisdom from within is true wisdom and divine magic.

It is said that in ancient times the gods of Nature willingly revealed themselves to the Theurgists, concealing nothing from these perfected men. When inspiration, intuition, imagination and reason are all trained, directed and united in one sublime faculty, he who possesses this faculty possesses the key to all natural mysteries.

We seek to achieve this high and glorious end according to the laws which have descended to us from those Hierophants of the old Wisdom Teachings, who are rightfully designated "princes of the Royal Secret." The philosopher seeks not worldly knowledge alone nor skill in worldly arts, but rather he aspires, if humbly now, to that greatest wisdom which "surpasseth understanding."

The Taoists, master metaphysicians of China, have curious collections of symbolic pictures which set forth with a peculiar force the mysteries of the Theurgic art. In a series of such paintings, the first shows a man trying to bridle a great black water-buffalo, in the second picture he is leading the animal by a halter, somewhat against its will. In the third picture, the head of the buffalo has turned white. And the fourth, fifth and sixth scenes the color disappears entirely, leaving the animal pure white. In the seventh scene, the white buffalo is shown led by the man across the clouds of heaven. In the eighth picture, the buffalo has entirely disappeared, and nothing but the man remains, walking in the sky. The series concludes with a ninth diagram. The man, the sky, stars, and all have disappeared and nothing remains but a large circle on a white field—the circle itself a symbol of eternal Tao.

The symbolism is of course evident to students of the ancient wisdom. The great black animal represents the material nature of man, this material nature including not only the physical body but all the materialistic impulses of the mind and the heart. In other words, the whole animal complex or focus which dominates in the unenlightened man.

Self-control is the first halter by which the animal is brought under the dominion of the true man. Through the disciplines of philosophy, the black buffalo gradually turns white, that is body becomes purified or regenerated, beginning with the head, for the mind is the first to perceive the task to be accomplished. The last parts to be redeemed are the chakras at the base of the spine which have control over the appetites and animalistic impulses. When this is finally accomplished, the white buffalo—the purified body—is transported to the Olympian spheres above the clouds. In other words, the body walks with God as described in the translation of Enoch.

Finally, the whole body is absorbed into consciousness. The animal disappears entirely and nothing remains but the meditating man, and the sky. Then comes the moment of the supreme Theurgy—the Nirvana of philosophy. The man, the sky, and all disappear, and nothing but absolute Truth remains. The Great Work has been completed.

Yours sincerely,

Manly P. Hall

New York, April 1, 1935

INTERESTING NEWS ITEMS

While in Paris, I made a careful examination of the celebrated Zodiac of Dendera. This famous stone planisphere was originally the ceiling of a small Egyptian temple in Dendera. The stone was for many years at Marseilles and was then brought to the Bibliotheque National. Recently, due to its great size, it was transferred to the hall of Egyptian monoliths at the Louvre. The planisphere of Dendera is the oldest example of a circular zodiac known. It is carved in shallow relief and includes not only the 12 zodiacal constellations but representations of the numerous constellations of the northern and southern hemispheres. According to the Egyptian authorities at the Louvre the Dendera zodiac was cut during the Ptolemaic period. The zodiac is of a brownish red stone about eight and a half feet square and eight to ten inches thick. It is exhibited horizontally on a low platform in the center of the gallery and has been examined and written about by many of the most celebrated authors on occult philosophy in the modem world. We have made arrangements with the authorities at the Louvre to have an exact replica of this zodiac cast from the original for the use of students in America. The transaction will be completed as soon as we have a proper place in which to display.

The Bibliotheque National of France is one of the most important libraries of the world. The manuscript collection alone comprises over a hundred thousand items, in every language of the ancient and modern world. In addition, the reading room of the manuscript section contains notes and catalogs classifying the contents of nearly all the important museums and libraries of Europe. This reading room is indeed a quaint spot. Due to incomplete indexing, the wealth of material which it contains is much of it comparatively inaccessible. This section of the library is profoundly influenced by the weather. There is no adequate electric lighting and on dull days it is impossible to find books in the stacks. Many of the best galleries and collections in Paris cannot be seen in the winter months. Even the great galleries of the Louvre are in constant twilight on an overcast day.

* * *

Something very interesting is taking place at the British Museum. The authorities of this institution are attempting to purchase the celebrated Codex Sinaiticus from the Russian government. This manuscript, which is the earliest known copy of the Gospels of the New Testament, was written in the fourth century of the Christian era. The Russian government has placed upon it the price of five hundred thousand dollars. The manuscript is on vellum in two-colored Greek characters, written four columns to the page. The work is of folio size, apparently about 12x15 inches to the leaf. The British Government has agreed to put up one-half of the purchase price, under the condition that the public will subscribe the other half. The manuscript is now being exhibited in a small case in the lobby of the museum, and beside it is a box in which those interested may drop their contributions "no matter how small." By this means some ten thousand dollars have already been raised and the fund is constantly increasing. Of importance to students of occultism is the fact that the Codex Sinaiticus contains many passages suppressed from the published Gospels. These passages in many cases greatly alter the significance of the text.

SOME PHILOSOPHICAL FRAGMENTS
NOTICE

THOSE interested in this work will be glad to know that we recently held a very successful exhibition of rare and curious occult books and manuscripts in the British Empire Building in Rockefeller Center, Radio City, New York City. In connection with this exhibit, which attracted wide interest, we delivered the following talk over radio station WMCA, New York City:

The Destruction of the Alexandria Library

It is generally acknowledged that the ancient Egyptians possessed an extraordinary knowledge of the arts and sciences. Their earliest Pharaohs were patrons of learning in all its branches. Their priests and philosophers were the most scholarly of men. The architecture of the Egyptians has awed the world for fifty centuries, and their wisdom in chemistry, anatomy, medicine and astronomy was no less amazing.

Under the dynasty of the Ptolemies, the city of Alexandria became a mecca for scholars. The studious of all nations congregated there to enjoy unparalleled opportunities for mental self-improvement. Poets, historians, philosophers and dramatists assembled in the city of the Ptolemies largely to consult the vast libraries which had been accumulated by the Pharaohs of this illustrious line.

Knowledge, like a magnet, draws more knowledge to itself, and by the second century, before the Christian era the city of Alexandria became a veritable metropolis of books. Its libraries are referred to in ancient documents as the glory of the world—the axis of the intellectual universe. In addition to numerous private libraries collected by specialists in various departments of learning, and the secret collections written in the hieratic glyphs of the priests, there were two immense public collections. The largest of these was the brachium which formed a branch of the national Museum of Antiquities, and contained some 490,000 papyri, vellums, tablets and inscriptions, magnificently arranged in the niches and wings of a great rotunda-like gallery. The second and smaller public collection, devoted almost exclusively to obscure forms of knowledge and therefore probably of greater practical value, was contained in the Temple of Serapis, the patron deity of the Ptolemies. This building called the Serapeum housed 42,800 rolls, preserved in fireproof containers shaped somewhat like buckets with tightly fitted lids. The various private collections brought the total number of priceless literary treasures in Alexandria to a figure exceeding one million DOCUMENTS.

It is difficult to compare this ancient collection with any modern library. Many institutions of the present day contain a larger number of books, as for example the British Museum, which has over 70 miles of bookshelves. But modern collections are mostly printed books of which there are numerous copies, comparatively inexpensive and easily secured. The Alexandrian collection was made up entirely of hand-written works, for the most part unique copies of the greatest antiquity, each of which today would be worth a king's ransom. There is not enough money in the world to buy the Alexandrian library if it existed today. When we realize that one fourth-century Greeks manuscript, the Codex Sinaiticus, is now being purchased by the British Museum for half a million dollars, we get some idea of the values.

The fate of the Alexandrian libraries is one of the greatest tragedies of history. In the first century B. C., Cleopatra contested with her brother for the throne of Egypt. Caesar ordered the burning of the fleet in the harbor of Alexandria. A strong wind rose, the fire reached the docks and spread. Before the conflagration could be checked, it destroyed the Brachium and the greater part of the city. When Cleopatra entered Alexandria under the favor of Caesar, she ordered herself carried to the ruins of the great library. The old accounts tell that she beheld a veritable mountain of charred manuscripts and rolls, and the Queen of the Sun cursed her ancestors that they had not made adequate provision to protect the library from fire. The burning of the Brachium was regarded by the Egyptians as a national disaster and by way of atonement Rome presented to Cleopatra several valuable collections of manuscripts which it had accumulated from conquered peoples. Mark Antony was especially active in the restoration of the Brachium.

The great Alexandrian libraries were a second time destroyed by Aurelian, about 273 A.D. The Serapeum was completely razed by the Christians in A.D. 389 by the Edict of Theodosius. The colossal statue of the weeping god Serapis, which stood in the midst of the Serapeum, was also demolished at this time. Alexandria never entirely recovered from this third catastrophe. The love of learning lingered on however until the last of the great collections was entirely wiped out by Amur the Saracen in A.D. 640. Thus perished the glory of the world, the sanctuary of the arts and sciences, mother of wisdom.

If we were asked to estimate what humanity has lost through the destruction of the Alexandrian libraries, we need only to say that after Alexandria came the Dark Ages—the total eclipse of essential learning. Today a hundred branches of art and science, philosophy and religion are laboring patiently and painfully to restore a body of knowledge which perished at the hands of ignorance and vandalism. The lost arts and sciences, the secrets of everlasting pigments, the mystery of malleable glass, the ever-burning lamps, and the transmutation of metals are among the minor losses. The greater tragedy is the loss of the histories of the antediluvian world—the beginnings of civilization—the origin of races, philosophies, religions and sciences—the secrets and accumulated knowledge of the lost Atlantis—and the story of its final destruction, when, according to the Troano Codex of the Mayans, it sank some 10 to 12 thousand years ago, carrying 60,000,000 souls to death in a single night!

Thus, the most precious secrets of human origin, to which we have recovered only the faintest clues, vanished away in smoke. Serapis, the sorrowful god, had the literature of a thousand generations for a funeral pyre.

But wisdom did not entirely die with the burning of its shrine. According to Theodas, faithful librarians and priests rescued a few of the most priceless of the manuscripts, hiding them in various places, and secreting a considerable number in underground temples in the Sahara Desert. Our great libraries and museums probably include among their various collections some mutilated fragments of this old collection that came to light in various excavations. But the important parts, if preserved, have not yet been rediscovered by the modern world.

There is a curious tradition to the effect that the priests and librarians of the Alexandrian institutions remained a group apart even after the destruction of their buildings. They gradually formed a community of their own and attempted to perpetuate orally and to set down from memory a part at least of the great teaching and literature which they had guarded and served for so many centuries. Thus, a certain part of the old knowledge is said to have been perpetuated through the centuries. There has always been a certain type of mind that loves to explore into the mysteries of life and nature. In the 15th, 16th, and 17th centuries, several groups of scholars appeared who attempted to piece together from tradition the lost learning of the ancients. Through the years darkened by religious and scientific bigotry and superstition, these research scholars worked secretly to restore what they believed to be the elements of essential knowledge. They did not, for the most part commit their findings to printed books, but, even after the invention of printing, they circulated their writings only among small groups of sympathetic thinkers.

Thus, manuscripts may be divided into two general periods. The first period, most generally collected and termed medieval, consists mainly of theological writings, illuminated Books of Hours, Palmisters and sermons. These books are collected mainly for their artistic merit but seldom for their contents. The second type of manuscripts, with the exception of a few isolated examples, belongs to a much later period and flourished most in the three centuries, which succeeded the discovery of printing. These manuscripts are seldom collected, and as far as we have been able to discover, there are no important collections of them in America.

These later manuscripts, written between 1450 and 1800, were not intended primarily as artistic or literary productions. Their artistic merit is of the accidents rather than the intention. These books, rolls, et cetera, are only collected by persons who actually desire to make use of their contents. They are not simply to be owned; they are to be studied and interpreted. Within them is to be found much real knowledge and many facts not generally known to even the scholars of the present day. The majority of these early modern manuscripts derived their inspiration from the classical collections of Alexandria. They attempt to bridge the centuries, to interpret the symbols and fables of the Egyptians and Chaldeans, to rediscover the scientific secrets of the Greeks and to render available to the modern world the profound lore of India and Arabia.

For the past fifteen years, it has been my purpose to collect for use in

America the curious manuscripts and early printed books produced by these secret groups of 16th to 18th century scholars whose findings and rediscoveries constitute the very foundation of modern science. The library was originally intended for private use, but it appears that an ever-increasing number of intelligent men and women are becoming interested in the sources of modern thought. For example, modern chemistry arose from the speculations of the medieval alchemists, and this collection contains many fine illumined alchemical manuscripts. The Hermetic wisdom of Alexandria gave rise to the biology and physics of today. The 16th century is the pivot between classical and modern learning, and the curious literary productions of this century are far greater in practical and intrinsic value than the theological Missals of the preceding centuries. It seems indeed a lamentable error of judgment that great modern institutions of learning, do not concern themselves more specifically with the examination and restoration of these systems of fundamental learning to which they owe their very existence.

Through the courtesy of the British Empire Building of Rockefeller Center, arrangements have been made for an exhibition of some 200 items from my personal collection of these curious books and manuscripts, many of them unique. In the collection are numerous items not to be found even in such libraries as the British Museum and the Bibliotheque National of Paris. We believe the exhibit will be unique not only for the strange documents with their extraordinary figures and diagrams but also in that it represents a valuable working library of source material which it is my intention to make available to the public.

Dear Friend,

With this month's issue, the first year of our Student's Monthly Letter is completed. We are happy that so many people have been interested in keeping in touch with our message through these little monthly talks. It has been a great joy to me to feel that through these letters; I have been in closer touch with our friends in all parts of the world.

In this first series, we have attempted to outline the first principles of philosophy. Already a great number of re-subscriptions have been mailed to us from those who desire that this monthly message shall continue to come to their homes. Therefore, beginning next month, we shall start a new series of 12 letters to be devoted to specific applications of the principles

New York, April 1, 1935

of occult philosophy to the spiritual problems which confront all students of the higher wisdom. The first section of each letter will be devoted to a fundamental problem of life in its spiritual aspect. We shall derive these problems from the countless questions that have been asked us during the years of our teaching. The second section of each letter will be devoted in part to specific questions sent in by subscribers to the letters, and in part to interesting sidelights on issues vital to our work, news, items, etc.

The first letter of the new series, beginning May 1st, will be devoted to answering the question of how the student shall contact bona fide sources of occult philosophy and spiritual instruction. We shall attempt to answer the questions: How shall I study, what shall I join, and how shall I know whether the claims of various individuals and organizations are true or false?

We hope that through this new series of letters, we can answer many of your pressing questions.

If you will fill in the enclosed form, these letters will continue to come to you each month. We are most grateful for your past support and look forward with sincere pleasure to our continued contact with you.

Very truly yours,

Manly P. Hall

AUTHOR AND MANAGING EDITOR

Darrell Jordan is an acolyte of the August Fraternity, former Noble Grand-IOOF and Freemason. He is also a member of the Theosophical and Philalethes Societies.

Darrell Jordan

BOOKS BY THE AUTHOR

- Illustrations of Masonry
- Surviving Document of the Widow's Son
- The Undiscovered Teachings of Jesus
- The Initiates
- Jefferson's Bible
- Master Masons Handbook
- Forgotten Essays - W.L. Wilmshurst
- Forgotten Essays - Waite
- Forgotten Essays - H. Stanley Redgrove
- The Writings of Sigismond Bacstrom M.D.
- Forgotten Essays – Reincarnation
- Masonic Writings of George Oliver
- Masonic Lectures by Wellins Calcott
- The Fellowcraft Handbook
- Secret Societies
- Vibration and Life
- Key to the Rosicrucian Characters
- The Revelation of John
- Life and the Ideal
- The Philosophical History of Freemasonry
- The Magic of the Middle Ages
- Musings of a Chinese Mystic
- The Life of the Soul
- Christian Mysticism
- Krishna and Orpheus
- The Eleusinian Mysteries & Rites
- The Crucifixion Letter
- The Mystic Key
- You Paid What?
- The Illustrated Pioneer History of the America
- Montana Freemasons 19th Century
- Washington Freemasons 19th Century
- Idaho Freemasons 19th Century
- Rock Metaphysics
- Emblems: Jean Jacque Boissard and Otto van Veen
- Emblems: Nicholas M. Meerfeldt
- Alchemy Art: Manly P. Hall
- Emblems: Manly P. Hall
- Alchemy Art & Symbols
- Splendor Solis

For the latest information, please visit author's book site: Parallel47North.com/collections/esoteric-books

If you have any question, suggestion, or feedback, please contact:

info@Parallel47North.com

Author and Managing Editor
MANLY P. HALL BOOK SERIES

All Seeing Eye Book Series

A Seeker of More Intelligent Life Book Series

Hand-drawn Illustration of Manly P. Hall and Book Cover Art by Jessica Naomi.

The Artist Portfolio: JessicaNaomiDesigns.com

www.ingramcontent.com/pod-product-compliance
Lightning Source LLC
Chambersburg PA
CBHW020309010526
44107CB00001B/43